Let The Woman Preach!

Messages From The Heart

By

Audrey Bowman

Let The Woman Preach!

Unless otherwise indicated, all scripture quotations are taken from the King James version of the Bible (KJV).

ISBN: 1-891773-41-0

Published by: ORMAN PRESS, INC.
4200 Sandy Lake Drive
Lithonia, GA 30038
770-808-0999
770-808-1955 Fax
www.ormanpress.com

Dedication

This book is dedicated to my
husband James for his
love, patience, and support
throughout our pilgrimage together;
to my two sons, Ephraim and Spencer;
and to my daddy, whose spirit
of preaching has made a
strong impact on my life and ministry.

Contents

Introduction

The question is not, "Does God call women to proclaim His Word?" Rather, the question is, "Does God speak through a yielded vessel?" Every now and then God touches the heart of one of His children and bids her to let Him speak through her. That heart is never the same and neither is the child of God.

Eight years ago I could no longer deny the call of God upon my life to speak forth His Word, even though He knew that the road would be a very difficult one. But God does not call us to cry out or draw attention to ourselves. He doesn't even require us to be sensational or witty or unique. He requires only that we be faithful.

This is a piece of my heart for the world to taste and see. My prayer is that God will use these messages again and again for His Kingdom's sake.

Lost And Found

Luke 15:11-24

I believe that almost everybody has lived through the traumatic experience of being lost—lost in the mall, lost on the highway, lost in a new city, or lost in the woods. We can experience a sense of lostness in a variety of ways in life: such as when we're caught in a dishonest act, or when we're lost in a lifestyle of immorality. Even depression and mental illness can be forms of lostness.

In this fifteenth chapter of Luke, Jesus describes three kinds of spiritual lostness. First, like sheep, we can be lost through sheer foolishness. We can sometimes just nibble our way, bit by bit, into a condition of lostness. Second, like the coin, we can become lost through the negligence and carelessness of other people. But the third kind of lostness that Jesus describes in this parable is a chosen and deliberate action. You know exactly what you're doing, and you just kick up your heels against God, your parents, or society; and just like the Prodigal Son, by choice you simply retreat to a far country. But the heart and soul of this parable is that the magnificent love of God, our Father, can defeat the foolishness of man, overcome the thoughtlessness of man, and conquer the deliberate rebellion of the human heart.

In this story, the tax collectors and notoriously wicked sinners were all coming near to hear Jesus. But the Pharisees and the scribes were acting indignant, and kept muttering and complaining about Jesus' willingness to accept, receive, welcome, and even sit down to eat with these wicked sinners. And that's why He told them this parable. Notice the singularity of the phrase "this parable." The lost sheep, the lost coin, and the lost son are actually three aspects of the same parable, each demonstrating how the love of God responds to our condition of lostness.

The third part of this parable then is the beautiful story of the Prodigal Son. If we are to really appreciate who we are in Christ and the kind of intimate love relationship that God desires to have with His people, then we have to grab hold of the manner in which Jesus began to tell this story. Verse eleven states that a certain man had sons—not that a certain king had subjects or that a certain landowner had slaves. The Fatherhood of God and the sonship of every believer are depicted against the close, personal community and communion of ordinary family life. Few things in the human experience are more precious and sacred than the relationship that God intends between a father and his son. And, if we look closely at this passage, we can see and understand that this certain man represents not only God Himself, but he represents the ideal human father—one who lives under the same roof as his family; a father who is at home with his children, maintaining a close and wholesome fellowship; a father who is accessible and approachable at all times; one who recognizes that growing up will involve some wise, as well as unwise decisions on the part of his children; a father who never forgets that a son will always be a son.

Now, most people would agree that a good home with loving, sacrificial parents does not necessarily guarantee that the children will not go astray. Many alcoholics were brought up by sober parents. A lot of drug addicts were brought up in drug-free home environments. But parents can free themselves from guilt and self-condemnation over a wayward child when we know in our hearts that we have done what God requires and we stand on the promise of His Word, that if you "train up a child in the way he should go: when he is old, he will not depart from it" (Proverbs 22:6).

And, I believe we can also agree that no two children will ever be exactly alike. Even twins have their own distinct identities. So, if children are different, then we can expect there to be differences in their needs. Further, the parent's manner of nurturing them might require differences in our approach to each individual child. A certain man had two sons.

It would not be expedient to deal with the older son in depth, because he requires a message all his own. But let's just take a look at the younger son and try to analyze him and his problems and how he tries to handle them. And I believe that the key to our understanding of this son's character can perhaps be found in the choice of adjectives that Jesus uses to identify and distinguish these two sons. This Prodigal Son is the younger son. That's a common way of distinguishing between two children, but they are not the only adjectives that Jesus could have used. For example, He could have referred to them as the first son and the second son; the good son and the bad son; the wise son and the foolish son; or even as the one son and the other son. But Jesus was not a man who made careless use of His words. And so, we have to conclude that there is some level of significance, some morsel of truth that is revealed in the fact that Jesus chooses to identify this particular son by saying that he was "the younger of them," even though research reveals that both of these sons were, in fact, adult men.

You see, there are certain qualities that seem to characterize youth and youthfulness. These characteristics that are expected to come with age don't always follow suit. That's why it's said of some people that they never grew up, because maturity is not counted in chronological age, but in wisdom. I don't think I'd be too far off if I said that some of us can remember the times when we were "younger" sons (at least we were younger than we are now); can claim some of the very same characteristics of this Prodigal, at some point in our lives; and can acknowledge the fact that at times we, too, were lost. But thank God that we have a wise and compassionate Father, whose love for His children outweighs our own sinfulness.

Well, in keeping with his immaturity, we see that the younger son got caught up in a selfish and self-centered state of mind. The first words that he spoke, in verse twelve, are "Give me." Not "lend me," but "give me." "I haven't earned it, but give me." "I don't deserve it, but give me." Not even "May I have" or "Would you please," but "Give me." Without any consideration or concern as to how such an action would affect his father's plans, or to what extent the estate itself would suffer, he demanded of his father, "Give me." The young and spiritually immature are so wrapped up in themselves and so unconcerned about anything other than what they can receive in life, that they become callous and indifferent to everything and everybody else, and fail to see the bigger picture. Their desires are selfish, their prayers are self-centered, their service is self-seeking, their giving is self-gratifying. What can I get out of this thing called Christianity? Give it to me. Give me my desires. Give me my recognition. Give me my position. Give me my seat. Give me my honor. Give me prosperity. Give me mine inheritance.

According to Deuteronomy 21:17, if a father had two sons, the elder son was entitled to two thirds of the estate, and the younger son was entitled to one third of the estate, after their father's death. And, we're told that it was not unusual for a man to distribute his estate before he died, if he so desired. But there's a cold and unfeeling tone in the son's demand. In effect, what he was saying was give me now the part of the estate I will get anyway when you're dead, and let me get on with my life. In other words, I want it all, and I want it now.

The Prodigal wanted his independence. He wanted to cut loose from his father's authority and responsibility, to do his own thing, to be his own man. Perhaps he found that his father's way of life was too demanding and required too much work and self-discipline. This life at home was just too restricting and too controlling, and he figured that his inheritance was a way out for him—a way that promised peace of mind, prosperity and freedom. Give me mine inheritance.

But look at the wisdom of the father's response. He has every right to say no. He knew for a certainty that his son was making a grave mistake. But a wise father also knows that sometimes his children have to learn their lessons in life the hard way. It's not the father's perfect will but his permissive will that leads him to divide up his living, knowing full well that this would not provide his son with life, because life exists not in the abundance of things. But love and life cannot be forced upon a son, not even by a loving father. And so, he gives his son his freedom and his possessions. With great anticipation and a false sense of security, the son takes off to make a life for himself in a far country.

The far country is not hard to find. Once you leave home, most any road will take you there. Almost anybody you know can tell you how to get there. Just about any time, day or night, you will find many travelers going in that same direction. And, if nothing else, the far country will attract you like a magnet. You can just coast downhill and get to the far country. You can float downstream and drift along through life, and you're sure to arrive. Or you can close your eyes and simply stumble in the darkness, but you will undoubtedly make it to the far country.

And when you get there, you're going to find, as the Prodigal discovers, that things are drastically different—nothing like what you're accustomed to at home. This place is full of bright lights and glitter, wild and extravagant parties, lust of the flesh and lust of the eyes. It's a place where men and women are lovers of themselves, and they're selfish and greedy. In this far country, the Prodigal discovers that money talks, and that it has the power to purchase temporary friendships. And he begins to like it there. But it's a dangerous thing—this far country—because there's always the potential for danger in a place where there's no responsibility, no expectations, no sacrifices, no standards to uphold, no deadlines to meet, no difficult decisions to make, nothing except what the world would call a good time—just moving from one high to the next.

But the main thing that we must never forget is that God is still in control, even in the far country. And there will come a time of famine when checks start bouncing and creditors start calling. There will surely come a time when resources dry up and investments don't pay off. When friends walk out and loneliness sneaks in. There will definitely come a time in the far country when the reality of a wasted life, wasted talents, and wasted opportunities will close in around us, and all that we had or thought we had will have been spent on riotous living. So, without the security that comes from God nor the honor and respect of our fellow men, we're forced to come to a rude awakening in the far country. That is, that we have compromised our principles, disgraced our good names, sold ourselves out to the lowest bidder, and we must now look up to see the pigs without God on our side—we're just LOST among swine. And to the Jew, the law said cursed is he who feeds the swine.

Sometimes we might have to spend time with pigs in order to recognize that we are not, and were never meant to be, pigs. When this young man was at home and in good fellowship with his father, he was a son. When he got to the far country and wasted all of his money and his potential, he was still a son. And now that he's hit rock bottom and is out there among the pigs, he's still not a pig, he's a son. This is the realization that comes to him and helps him to be able to come to himself. What Jesus is saying in this story is that as long as a son is in rebellion against God, he is not really himself, and never can be, until he's back home with the Father. To try to be something other than who we are in Christ is insanity, it's crazy, it's unreal, and it's sin.

Now, this prodigal's coming to himself is what we want to take a closer look at, because coming to oneself is the beginning of being found. Because repentance begins with a change of mind, this keen awareness; this consciousness of who we are (and whose we are); this return to a sound mind is the beginning of sanity (and of reality) and marks the first step toward being found. The Holy Spirit makes His first appeal to a man's intelligence. He works on our intellect and brings us to the point where we're forced to think things over. We begin to mentally analyze the situation. In our minds, we gather up all the pieces of the puzzle and look at all angles of our circumstances, and if we allow ourselves to concentrate long and hard enough, then we're most likely to come to some intelligent conclusions about the matter.

So we see the Prodigal Son, in verse seventeen, engaged in the first step toward true repentance: there's a change taking place in his mind. His thoughts were of his father's generous provisions: that he had bread to spare. He meditated upon that sense of belonging that he once knew. He remembered the feeling of being a family, and fellowshipping together among the Father's servants. He rehearsed in his mind the great provisions of love and joy and peace that he knew in his father's house. And then he went deeper in thought as he began to compare that with his own predicament: "I perish." In other words, "My life is wasting away; my self-esteem is withering up; my hope is vanishing; my future is fading away; decay has set in on all of my dreams; I have no vision and without a vision, I perish."

The Prodigal Son then moved on to the second step of repentance: the point of conviction. Conviction is a sign that we're beginning to sober up. Conviction is that friction on the inside that rubs against the grain of our sinful inclination, overpowers every evil intent, and then brings us to the point where there is now some clarity of understanding and soundness in judgment—judgment that's free from any kind of emotional influence. When we have been thoroughly convicted, we're able to come face to face with the ugly reality of our own lostness, and there's no question about what to do, what course of action we have to follow. You see, it's not enough to merely think about our sins or to intellectualize them, we have to be totally convicted of our sins, and then we have to be humble enough to follow the leading of good conscience, because a change of mind ought to lead a sinner to a change of heart. That's conviction—having a change of heart.

Out there in the far country, the Prodigal Son reaches the point of conviction in his life. The desire and longing to return to his father is gnawing deep down in his heart, creating a void, a chasm, a hunger and a thirst that cannot be satisfied with anything other than the Living Bread and the Living Water.

But the work of repentance is not yet complete. Reflection of our sins should lead to conviction of sin, but without confession of sin, there's no true repentance. And 1 John 1:9 says, "If we confess our sins, he is faithful and just to forgive us our sins, and to cleanse us from all unrighteousness." We can't afford to overlook the fact that true confession, the kind that we see in this parable, will always require and compel us to rise up and return—to get up out of the pigpen and take off in the opposite direction. The Father knows that our confession is genuine only when He sees appropriate action—when He observes us actually turning from our wicked ways. We can't just say "Yes, I did it," and then go about our business. We can't just acknowledge the fact of sin without completely turning from sin to God. Turning to God is necessarily a turn in an upward direction. The Prodigal says to himself in verse eighteen, I will arise from the stench of this pigsty, and I will go to my father.

And what I like about our Heavenly Father is that His forgiveness is both complete and unconditional. He's not like some people who say that they forgive, then they continue to hold your sins up to your face. When God forgives, He wipes the slate clean and He acts as if the thing never happened. So that means that we don't have to be afraid to hold back anything in our confession to the Father. It means that there's no need to try to clean ourselves up before we go to Him. Our efforts would be futile, even if we tried, because all of our righteousness is as filthy rags in the sight of God. It's foolish to try to impress God with filthy rags. All we have to do is to come just as we are. The cleansing will take place when we get there.

Let's take one final look at the Father's response to his wayward, wasteful son. First of all, he accepted his son before he gave a verbal confession. That tells us that this father was well acquainted with the heart of his own son.

A loving, caring father, one who has spent time with and has invested himself in the life of his son, has sufficient knowledge of the true nature of his child. This father knew that any of his sons were subject to sink into the pigsty of sin. But he also had full knowledge of the fact that no true son of his could stay there for very long, because HIS sons didn't like pigpens. His true sons cannot remain comfortable and content wallowing among hogs. The father knew that his son could never be happy anyplace but home; he could never be completely satisfied anyplace but home; his true son could never find spiritual fulfillment anyplace else but home. He would never find peace of mind and lasting prosperity, anyplace else but home. A father knows this about his son, and that's why this father was constantly on the lookout for his son to come on home. All the while the Prodigal Son had been living it up in the far country. Back at the house his loving father had been patiently waiting and watching. He was just waiting for his son's stomach to get hungry enough. He waited until his clothes became ragged enough. He just waited for his body to get dirty enough. He waited for his son's heart to get broken enough. He just waited and watched, because a father is well acquainted with his own son.

And not only that, but the father in this story had to be well acquainted with the dichotomy of sin and repentance. In other words, he had to have full knowledge of the process that leads us into the pigpen, as well as a full understanding of the process that leads us out of the pig-pen and into a condition of full repentance. He understood what it means to be lost and found. And that's why his feet were quick to start running, because when the father spotted his son from afar off, he was wise enough to know that had his son not gone completely through the process of repentance; had he not made a clean break and a complete turnaround, the son would never have made it that close to home.

He was certain enough about his sons full repentance, that he gave orders to the servants: "Bring out the best robe so I can clothe him in my righteousness. Bring out some shoes for his feet, so that everybody will know that he's been restored to the honor that all sons receive. And then put my signet ring on his finger as a testimony of his position of authority. And then last, but not least, kill the fatted calf, because my son has returned to me hungry, and I intend to feed him until he wants no more. It's time to be happy and make merry because my son has been resurrected. He WAS dead and is alive again; he was lost but now...."

The Need For A Second Touch

Mark 8:22-26

There are two things to be noted about the miracle of this text: it was recorded only by Mark and it intentionally occurred in stages. It is this second peculiarity that attracts our attention more, because the method of healing that Jesus used, in this case, was distinctively different from that of His other miracles. To get an understanding of the reason for the Lord doing what He does, we have to get a grip on the divine purpose for the healing in the first place. You see, this was more than a healing miracle—it was also an object lesson. The Lord had been trying to get a spiritual point across to His disciples, and it was not surprising that they had been missing the point. They had not connected with the spiritual import of the Master's words. It's not surprising because on so many other occasions, we see their confusion about spiritual things. They missed the point when Jesus declared that He and the Father are one. They missed the point when He talked of His suffering and death. They missed the point right on through His death, burial, and resurrection—not because the Lord didn't teach them well enough, but because their human minds were unable to grasp spiritual things. Jesus Himself sighed with frustration that His very closest disciples, who were privileged to walk with God in the flesh, and talk with Him, and eat and sleep with Him, and listen to what He had to say, and see what He did, were still lacking spiritual understanding. They were blind and didn't know it.

You see, blindness is much more than a physical malady. One can be in the dark about a whole lot of things. Blindness can refer to the inability to carry out something, because of the lack of knowledge and experience; to be ignorant and void of truth. But, "to see" means to have clarity about a subject; to be equipped with the faculties of comprehension and awareness; to understand.

Mark says that it was after the feeding of the four thousand, with seven small loaves of bread, that the Pharisees came out and started an argument with Jesus. They wanted to test Him, by asking for a sign from heaven. But Jesus refused to give them one. Then He turned away, got into a boat and crossed over to the other side of the lake. His disciples were with Him, but they had forgotten to bring enough bread with them. They had only one small loaf, and they were discussing this issue among themselves when Jesus spoke these words to them: Beware of the leaven of the Pharisees and of Herod. Again we notice that the disciples are missing the point, because they concluded that the Lord was chiding them for not bringing along enough bread. Well, for heaven's sake, the man had just performed a bread miracle. He had just multiplied seven loaves right before their eyes, and there was bread in abundance. But now that they're in the boat with the Living Bread, they completely miss the point: If Jesus could feed four thousand, then surely He was capable of feeding them. So the Lord turned to His disciples in verse seventeen and said, "Why are you talking about not having any bread? Don't you understand? Are your minds still closed? Are your eyes blind and your ears deaf? Don't you know what I'm talking about?"

Have you ever attempted to converse with people on a spiritual level, only to discover that they just keep missing the point? Carnal minds cannot discern the things of the Spirit. Don't you get frustrated sometimes, when you try to communicate the things of God to folk who have been around the church for years and years, yet there is no connection made, and they go off still confused and unable to comprehend? Jesus experienced the same thing with His disciples. So then, it is possible to be exposed to the things of the Spirit and still be spiritually blind. It is possible to hear the Words of the Spirit and still be spiritually deaf, because our minds are closed and our hearts are hardened to the truth of God.

So as divine providence would have it, once they got to shore and began heading toward Bethsaida, a group of people brought a man who was physically blind to Jesus, and the Lord used this miracle opportunity to demonstrate a spiritual truth and spiritual values to His disciples. Notice that the blind man did not come to Jesus on his own, but he was brought by his friends. In other words, his presence was not an expression of his own faith, but of the faith of his friends. This teaches us the value of true friendship. True friends are those whose eyes are already open and who can see Jesus for themselves. A blind person is always in good company when he's around others who can see. The friends of the blind man knew by experience the advantages of sight. And they loved and cared for him enough to desire a better life for him. So they brought him to Jesus, because they had enough faith to believe that He could do for him what nobody else had been able to do. No doubt the blind man had been a burden to his family and friends, and they had become a crutch for him. He had become dependent upon other people's time, energy, and efforts. Our deficiencies, our handicaps, and our hangups always affect other people. Thus, the blind man's deliverance would be their deliverance as well.

We also see in this verse the value of intercessory prayer. It says here that they besought Jesus, they begged and pleaded with Him, they prayed that the Lord would touch their friend. We need to pray for those who are spiritually blind to the truth, and we need to be perceptive of their spiritual needs so that we can be specific in our prayers on their behalf. The friends in this story asked specifically for a touch. This man's healing could have taken place at a distance, but his friends perceived that what he really needed the most was a touch from the Lord. He was without his sense of sight. It's a fact that when you lose one of your senses, the others become more acute. To a blind person, reality comes through points of contact. They perceived that his faith would be activated if Jesus would only touch him.

And they were right about that, because Jesus responded to their specific request. In verse twenty-three, He took the blind man by the hand. This was an act of servanthood on the part of Jesus. He could have commanded one of His disciples or one of the man's friends to be responsible for his relocation. But the Lord chose to do it Himself. No act of service is too low or too small for Jesus to get personally involved in. Through this act of servanthood, we learn the value of intimacy with Jesus. He then took the blind man by the hand. Think about what it means to hold hands. It's different from shaking hands. A handshake is a point of contact, but it's a short-lived experience. It doesn't last very long. But the holding of hands implies an intimacy between the two parties by mutual consent. Handholding denotes a partnership, a spirit of cooperation and commitment. It's a symbol of our walk with God. You see, in order to advance spiritually; in order to receive a blessing from the Lord; in order to be saved, set free and delivered from our physical and our spiritual bondage, we have to walk hand in hand with the Master. (We have to be willing to do our part, because God is faithful to do His.) There's something special about having your hand in Jesus' hand. There's security in His hands. There's healing in His hands. There's wonder working power in His hands. Precious Lord, take my hand. It's a blessing of great magnitude for a blind man to be able to put his hand in the hand of Jesus.

And so, hand in hand, the Lord led the blind man outside of the village. In other words, He took the man away from the crowd. There's no doubt in my mind that this miracle could have taken place right there on the spot. But Jesus is always very deliberate and intentional in what He does. The Lord is not limited in His methodology. He doesn't have to do the same thing in the same old way for everybody. It depends upon the individual circumstance and the need of the hour. Sometimes He heals when people come up and touch Him. Other times He heals from miles away. Sometimes, He merely speaks a word of healing. But this particular man had a special need. For this reason, the Lord led him away from the village. There are times in our lives when we need to get away from the crowd and stand before the Lord. There can be too much static and distractions from the crowd. There may be Pharisees in the crowd, seeking to put a stumbling block in your way. Some people in crowds are just curiosity seekers who will try to get into your business and spread gossip about you. And if Jesus had performed this miracle before the crowd, in the way that He did, some people would have run off with only half the story. They may have concluded that the Lord didn't even know what He was doing out there. Everybody in the crowd is not likely to have the same mission and motives that you have. There may be some people in the crowd who are not for you, but against you. When you're spiritually blind, and your deepest need is to receive your sight, the Lord may have to take you by the hand and lead you away from the crowd. *Lord help me!*

Another reason for this decision may have had something to do with the faith of the blind man. His ability to see the presence of a crowd could have clouded his mind about who was actually effecting his healing. It might have made him suspicious of what was being done to him and how it was being done. So, moving him away from the crowd would serve the purpose of increasing the certainty of Jesus as the sole deliverer. It served to eliminate all other possibilities. Our God is a jealous God, and it grieves Him when He works miracles in our lives, and then we proceed to give credit to something or somebody else. Sometimes when the Lord is about to perform spiritual surgery, He is careful to eliminate all other possibilities, so that we can know, without a doubt, it was nobody but Jesus.

The next thing that Mark wants us to focus our attention upon is the method that Jesus used in restoring sight to the blind man. In that same verse, we're told that He spat on the man's eyes, and then put His hands upon him. This gives us a little more insight as to how the Lord deals with us as individuals. Wherever we are in our knowledge and understanding of spiritual things, wherever we are in our level of faith and on the basis of our own belief systems, Jesus meets us where we are, in order to bring us to where we ought to be. You see, the saliva itself is not necessary for the man's healing to take place. But there was a common belief among that culture in the healing powers of saliva. It was used in a number of ways. For example, if a person were to burn his fingers, he would immediately put them into his mouth—and the saliva would help to cool things off a bit. We might even speculate that this common practice had proven to be an unsuccessful remedy. The missing ingredient in the treatment of saliva was the hand of Jesus. Whatever we might attempt to do to secure the abundant life for ourselves is useless, unless the hand of God is upon it. It takes the Spirit of God to activate spiritual things.

Now we come to the climax of the story and the spiritual principle that Jesus wanted to teach His disciples. He asked the man a question that He already knew the answer to: "Can you see anything," or as some versions have it, "What is it that you see?" It's an opportunity for the man that was blind to testify for himself, but it goes a little deeper than that. It also serves as a demonstration to the disciples of their special need for humility, and honest confession about their own spiritual condition.

Here's a man who has been touched by Jesus. There's no doubt about that. And suddenly he realized that he was not totally blind anymore. But by the same token, he also understood that something was still lacking in his vision. His healing was not complete. And he made an honest confession about what he was able to see and not see. He says, "I see men, but they look like trees, walking." (I hope His disciples are not missing the point here.) To confess that you've had a great spiritual experience but that you're still not completely whole is a mark of true humility. You see, there are some people who receive that initial touch from Jesus, and then they go off professing that they have it all, they know it all, they can do it all, they see it all so clearly now, when what they see is men looking like trees, walking. (Glory to God!)

As disciples of Jesus, there is evidence within us and all around us that indicates that some obstruction is still blocking our view. If we could see things as clearly as we ought to see them, then men would take their rightful

unconditional

place as the spiritual heads of their families, and wives would be submitting themselves to somebody who loves them, as Christ loves the Church. If we, as disciples, could see all that God purposes for us to see right now, then the church would be taking the Gospel out there in the community, trying to rescue people who are dying and going to hell, instead of waging war on the Body. If the people of God had 20/20 spiritual vision today, we wouldn't be robbing God of His resources, and we would be getting ourselves out of debt, owing no man anything, except to love Him. If we could truly see things as God sees them, then we would set our affections on things above, and we wouldn't be so impressed with outward appearances. We'd be more concerned about the condition of the inner man. Yes, we've been touched by God, all right, but our spiritual vision is still somewhat cloudy.

Thank God that this man was honest enough to admit that he was much better off than he used to be, but that his present condition was far less than what he desired. "I'm looking at something, but it looks like something else. My view is distorted, unclear and uncrystalized." Do you see anything? What is it that you see? The Lord is asking. "Well, I see people, but I'm not sure what their motives are." "I see my family, but it's not so clear how much they love me." What is it that you see? "I see the church, but I can't quite make out where I fit in. I'm not sure about my purpose and place in the Body." "I see a generation of young children gone astray, but I can't discern clearly their potential." What is it that you see? "Oh, I see God's love, but His forgiveness escapes me." "I see the cross, but I can't quite focus on the crown. I see nothing now as I ought to see it. My spiritual insight is coming up short. Even though I have been touched by the hand of Jesus, there are still so many things that I do not understand. They're not clear to me right now. My spiritual vision is both limited and cloudy." As the Apostle Paul would say it's like looking through a glass darkly. And that's the point that the Lord Jesus was trying to make to His disciples. That's the purpose of this miracle. He wants us to get a clear understanding of the fact that our spiritual growth and development comes in stages. It's a process that takes place over a period of time. As our faith increases, God is able to reveal more and more of Himself to us.

So, then, what do we do about our partially blind condition? Will we be content with only the knowledge and insight that we have now? Will we continue to stumble around and over the blessings that God wants us to enjoy? Are we content to just keep missing the point? Jesus says we don't have to. If we had enough faith to receive that first touch, His Word will lead us from faith to faith. And by faith we can allow Him to touch us a second time, and then touch us again and again and again until our healing is complete and our eyes of spiritual understanding have been opened and enlightened by our faith in Him and by the touch of the Master's hand. Touch me again, Lord Jesus. For He who has begun a good work in you is faithful to continue it, until Christ comes the second time.

A Resurrection Faith

1 Corinthians 15:58

Notice that this verse begins with the word "therefore." I heard somebody say once that anytime you come upon the word "therefore," always back up to find out what it's "there for." So, if we would back up to the beginning of Chapter Fifteen, we discover that Paul was defending the doctrine of the resurrection of the dead: clearing up a misconception; putting a stop to false doctrine that so often creeps into the church; and then reestablishing sound doctrine, that had already been taught and accepted as truth by the church.

Sisters and brothers, I want to suggest early on that the church is in a dangerous position when we allow false doctrine to creep in and prevail within our ranks, without somebody speaking up about it and then doing something to stop it. The danger is that if this kind of thing goes unchecked, uncorrected—if it goes too far—it begins to spread like a disease, and pretty soon, the church of God loses its identity. Even though we might continue to do some helpful, needful things; even though we might continue to support good causes and promote good principles, the church that bases good works upon false doctrine would no longer be the church.

We don't need to think that the Corinthian church was the only church with this problem. We can't afford to believe that the church around the corner is the only church with this problem. Every church needs to be on constant guard and continual watch because there are so many ways that we can get sidetracked in our beliefs, especially during the infant stages of spirituality. What we'll find is that false doctrine will stunt our spiritual growth, such that we're still on milk when we ought to have moved on toward meatier matters of the faith. We'll find that we're still dabbling in childish things when we should have grown up and put childish things away.

The church at Corinth was established by Paul during his second missionary journey. He stayed with them for almost two years, laying a solid foundation for their faith and planting good seeds among them. Apollos came after him, and Peter also stopped by and ministered to them. But somewhere along the way, certain misconceptions, misunderstandings, and misconduct had been allowed to creep in, and the church at Corinth became sidetracked in their beliefs.

One way to get off the right track is to succumb to worldly influences brought into the church by new converts. As these influences begin to rise up in those who hold positions of leadership, the weak folks (those who are trusting, unsuspecting, and insecure) will be overshadowed in their own beliefs, and become like children playing with toys they don't quite know how to operate. But instead of checking out the instruction manual for themselves, they're taken in by these new converts, these carnal minded Christians who say, "Oh, this is how we did that last year, and it worked so well at the office or in my civic association, so surely it ought to work well in my church."

Tied in to all of this is the fact that so many church people just refuse to study God's Word for themselves. They would rather depend on what certain other people believe. And if he/she says that's the way it is, then that must be the way it is. It's amazing how people of worldly influence can come into our churches and set themselves up as the standard for others to follow.

Another way for the church to get sidetracked, as we look at the example of the Corinthians, is for its members to fall into sin, and then develop such a tolerance for sin that the clear commands of God's Word become twisted and distorted—so that nobody's toes are stepped on and nobody's feelings get hurt. And we think that if we just ignore it long enough, it'll go away. We begin making excuses for sin, and the church begins missing the mark.

So the Apostle Paul, in his role as a preacher and teacher of the Gospel, under divine inspiration and with the boldness given through the unction of the Holy Ghost, proceeded to set things back in order in the church. After all, it was his job, his responsibility, his charge, and his commission to proclaim, to protect, and to preserve the purity of the Gospel of Jesus Christ. And no other Gospel did he preach except the same Gospel that he himself received—that the Lord Jesus, the Son of God, died for our sins, according to the scriptures, was buried, and rose again the third day. We all know that to be the Gospel, the full Gospel, and nothing else but the Gospel.

But there were folks in the church at Corinth who were a lot like so many of us are today. You see, they had accepted this Gospel at one time, but they never grew up spiritually; and like children, they allowed themselves to be tossed to and fro, to be carried away with every other wind of doctrine. (Some of you may know some people like that.) At one time the Corinthians had no problem accepting by faith the truth of the divinity of Jesus—that Jesus is the Son of God. But then something changed. Something happened that allowed doubt to enter into their minds.

Perhaps some of them went to college, to the finest educational institutions, and became exposed to the greatest philosophers of all times. Or maybe they went to spend time with family or friends and had an opportunity to attend their worship services. Or they might have been listening to an early morning talk show on the radio. Or it might just be that they were sitting around one day at the barber and beauty shop while a serious discussion was going on (you know, everybody giving their opinions!) and they came away with the false notion that Jesus was nothing more than a man. They might acknowledge that He lived a good life, that He went about the seashores of Galilee helping a lot of people, yet He was only a man. Human, worldly intelligence shuts the door on the reality of a babe being born to a virgin. So what they had once accepted by faith is now regarded as foolishness. Jesus was a good man they say, but like all men, when it was His time to die, He died, and that's the end of the story.

How wretched and miserable we all would be if this were true. How lost and without hope we Christians would be to fasten our faith to, fix our minds upon, and focus our energy toward a philosophy or a doctrine that dies when we die! But Paul had to jolt the Corinthians back to their senses and remind them that there is no Gospel without the resurrection. To believe that God raised His Son from the dead, that His death gave us the victory over sin, and that His resurrection gave us the victory over death is not an option for believers. Paul says that if we don't believe in the resurrection, then we are the most miserable of all of God's creatures, because not only have we made God a liar, but we ourselves have been deceived. If there is no such thing as the resurrection of the dead, then our faith is faulty, our hope is helpless, and our joy is unjustified. If Christ be not risen from the dead, then we don't need our Bibles—we're just wasting our breath when we pray—and the church is nothing but a fraud, because everything that we do is done through the power of a resurrected Savior. Who has bewitched you? It's elementary to have to deal with you on this level of spiritual understanding, but let me remind you that Peter, James, and about five hundred other believers saw the Master in person. And I myself, who might be counted the least of the Apostles—I saw Him for myself.

Brothers and sisters, you have to see Jesus for yourself to know that He is not dead. He's alive forevermore because He lives within my soul. And if you believe that, then your actions ought to line up with your beliefs. So then, we get to the word "therefore": The conclusion of the matter is this. Since you know this to be true, then you ought to be steadfast, unwavering, unfaltering in your faith of the Gospel that you heard me preach. Hold on to your faith. Don't let anybody take it away from you. For without faith, it's impossible to please God. Somebody said faith is believing without seeing and going without knowing. That means that I can't let my circumstances dictate my faith. But faith is what helps me to look beyond my circumstances and sustains me through every trial and tribulation. Faith enables me to stay calm in the midst of my storms and have peace in the midst of confusion. That's why Paul tells us to be steadfast in our faith.

Not only that, we also need to be unmovable in our hope. Faith and hope will always go together. We have to recognize that our hope is not built on anything that we've done. It's not built on our church membership, nor on the fact that we read our Bibles and say our prayers. But our hope is built on nothing less than Jesus' blood and His righteousness. The foundation of the hope that we have in our hearts is the resurrection of the Lord Jesus. And since we know that Jesus got up from the grave, we also know that the grave will not be our final resting place. That's not just wishful thinking for a Christian, that's a holy expectation, a blessed assurance that is rooted and grounded in faith.

Finally now, with faith on one side and hope on the other, Paul tells us what we as Christians ought to be doing. Any believer who is steadfast in faith and unmovable in hope ought not be found just sitting back, waiting for the Lord's return. It's hard to understand how so-called Christians can be content to just drop in on Sunday mornings and critique the worship experience, then go on about their business until they decide to drop in again—never demonstrating a genuine desire to be about the Father's business. Paul tells us that if our faith and our hope are in tact, then we ought to be abounding in the work of the Lord. It doesn't mean that we're to abound every now and then, or one or two times a year, or only on special occasions: it means we are to always abound in the work of the Lord until He comes again.

We have to be ever so mindful that the work we abound in is not our own work, but the work of the Lord. It's so easy to be impressed with the activities and "busyness" of today's church life. We can get sidetracked with church work and not even recognize the real work of the church. Jesus said, "I must work the works of him that sent me, while it is (still) day" (John 9:4a). It won't always be day, for the night cometh when no man can work. So it behooves every one of us to make the most of our time doing the Lord's work. If we examine the work that Jesus did, we won't find that He ever sold a raffle ticket for the Kingdom. We won't find that He ever sponsored a pageant or a contest or a fashion show for the Kingdom. If we search our Bibles, we won't find Jesus organizing birthday clubs for the Kingdom. My Bible tells me that Jesus went about doing good. When He set out on a mission to seek and to save people who were lost, He was doing good. When He went forth preaching and teaching the Kingdom of God, He was doing good. When He met the needs of the poor folk in the community; when He healed the sick, raised the dead, and gave sight to the blind, He was doing good. When He took time out to nurture the outcast and the downtrodden, when He opened eyes of understanding and filled hearts with love, Jesus was doing good. So then, everybody who has faith in the Lord Jesus Christ ought to be about the business of doing all the good we can for as many people as we can, while we have a chance.

But don't be surprised by the opposition you have to face when you're doing the Lord's work. Don't be discouraged by the persecution you have to encounter when you're doing the Lord's work. Don't give up and quit because of the rejection you're bound to feel when you're doing the Lord's work. Just keep on abounding, because the joy of it all is in the promise of His Word: when we're doing His work, then our labor is not in vain in the Lord.

I'm glad about that. It's just good to know that our faith is not in vain. No prayer that's been offered up in faith will ever be in vain. No song sung to the glory of God will ever be in vain. No mountain of opposition that we've had to climb will ever be in vain. None of the criticism that we've had to listen to will ever be in vain—because the Bible tells us that one of these old days (we know not the day nor the hour) the Lord Himself shall descend from Heaven with a shout. And at the sound of the last trumpet, the dead in Christ shall rise and those of us who still remain will be caught up to meet Him in the air. That's good enough reason to hold on to our faith!

After The Storm, Then What?

Mark 5:1-9

The Lord Jesus called His twelve disciples unto Him and ordained them, that they should be with Him and that He might send them forth to preach, to have power to heal sickness, and to cast out devils. But in order for the disciples to fulfill their calling and to be effective in the ministry that they had been given, there had to be adequate preparation. So the Lord Himself became their teacher. He taught them both in public and in private. He taught them by precept and by example. He taught them through parables and through personal experiences. For Jesus knows that no matter how much knowledge you might have in your head, there can be no authority, no authenticity in your ministry until you have experienced some things for yourself.

After ministering the Word to the multitudes, Jesus withdrew himself from the crowd and directed His disciples to go with Him to the other side of the Sea of Galilee. He obviously needed a time of rest and recuperation. You see, true ministry exacts virtue from the minister. Spiritual energy is depleted after a while, and there must be a time of refueling and regrouping, a time of refreshing of the mind, body, and spirit.

This is an important part of the teaching and preparation given to the disciples. And there's a lesson to be learned here for everybody in the service of the Lord. Regardless of the demands of the crowds, wisdom dictates that we periodically withdraw ourselves in order to renew, replenish, and refocus our thoughts on God. And so, after a period of intense teaching and preaching and healing, Jesus and His disciples entered a ship and set sail for the other side of the sea.

It was a relatively short trip to make: the Sea of Galilee is only about thirteen miles long and about seven miles wide. The Bible doesn't say how long they had been out there before a fierce storm arose and began to beat forcefully against the sides of the ship, causing the disciples to fear for their very lives. This had to be a pretty rough storm because these men were experienced sailors; there were some professional fishermen on that boat. And yet, they were intimidated by the waves and the winds of this mighty storm. Chances are that they had never anticipated a storm ahead. There had been no indicators in the sky or in the measures of barometric pressure. So this was an unexpected storm.

Those of us who have had a few experiences on the sea of life can attest to the fact that there are times when we see the warning signs of bad weather approaching, and we brace ourselves for the turbulence ahead. But then there are other times when everything seems to indicate smooth sailing for a while, so we plunge ahead with no real expectation that we're moving into a storm. Sometimes the Lord will allow the unexpected to rise up and to challenge our faith, and to test our spiritual preparedness, so that he can manifest Himself to us at another level and get us ready for a greater dimension of service to Him. Sometimes the Lord just needs to get us to a place where we're at our wit's end; we're at the end of our ropes; we've exhausted all of our human resources; we've tried everything we could think of, and the only thing left to do is to go down on our knees and call upon the name of the Lord.

You see, the basic lesson to be learned about every storm of life, whether expected or unexpected, is that God always has a reason for everything that He allows to come upon and against us. There is always purpose in our pain. For according to scripture, even storms work together for good, to them that love the Lord and who are the called according to His purpose. But it's very likely that His purpose for the storm will not be revealed to us while we're going through it. Yet, if we remain faithful to Him during the storm, we're sure to discover His purpose once we make it to the other side.

Let's look at the action that occurs on the other side of this storm. We're told in verse one of Chapter Five that once Jesus and His disciples made it to shore, immediately "there met Him out of the tombs a man with an unclean spirit." That's the secret of the storm. It was merely a part of the disciples' Christian education. The storm had been a necessary course in faith stimulation. On the front side of the storm, they had sat under the powerful and authoritative teachings of the Master and were astonished at His doctrine. They had witnessed some of His healing miracles—such as the healing of Simon's mother-in-law, a leper, and one sick of the palsy. They even witnessed the power of Jesus over an unclean spirit in Capernaum. But that was entry-level stuff. That was Faith 101. The storm itself had ushered the disciples into a deeper level of faith, because when the storm was over, they had to marvel at the kind of man Jesus was, that even the winds and the waves obeyed His voice.

We need to come to the understanding that that's how this Christian journey is supposed to be. We ought to be growing deeper and deeper in the things of God. We ought to know God better now than we did when we first believed. We ought to be expecting more from God and attempting greater things for Him as we move from faith to faith and from glory to glory. And that's the purpose of every storm. It's like climbing Jacob's ladder, knowing that every round goes higher and higher.

Now, as soon as this storm was over, and Jesus and His followers made it to dry land, they realized that the storm had come simply to prepare them for an even greater ministry opportunity: a man with an unclean spirit. But this time it's a case of extreme demon possession. There are so many Christians today, sad to say, who don't believe that demons exist. And that's why they live such defeated lives. For if Satan is the god of this world (and he is), if he is the prince of darkness (and he is), then that means that he's the head of something. When you're the head of something, that automatically implies that there are subordinates working under you who are subject to your command. So a demon is nothing more than a messenger of Satan whose job is to influence us to disobey God. As believers, we're actually up against demonic spirits and demonic activity on a daily basis.

Let's look at verse nine for a better description of the demoniac's condition. We find here that Jesus was not inquiring about the identity of the man. He questioned the identity of the spirit within the man when He said, "What is thy name?" The voice of the spirit answered back: "My name is Legion, for we are many." In Roman antiquity, it took anywhere from two thousand to six thousand soldiers to make up a legion. But the point is not to count them and come up with an exact number. The point is simply to illustrate to us that if we're going to do spiritual warfare, we've got to know that there are many unclean spirits out there and that they all have a name.

Time will not permit us to name them all. However, to get a clearer picture of the wretched condition of this demoniac, so that we might grasp the spiritual understanding that even though Jesus and His disciples have just survived one storm only to encounter another storm raging on the inside of this man, let's conduct a partial "roll call" of these unclean spirits.

What is thy name? My name is Fear. My job is to keep this man in a constant state of apprehension. To keep him uneasy about launching out into the deep waters of faith. I see to it that he's overly concerned about what people might say about him. He's scared to death that he might not be successful or popular. He can't stand to be embarrassed or rejected or laughed at. So he would rather do nothing for the Lord and to remain in bondage to fear.

What is thy name? My name is Complacency. My assignment is to keep this man satisfied with what he's already done for God's Kingdom. I just reassure him that only the bare minimum is necessary to please God. "That's good enough," I tell him. "You've already prayed enough and worshipped enough and given enough and done enough things to make a good showing on Judgment Day." And I'm doing a fine job with him too, because now he's too lazy to get down on his knees and pray, too lazy to open up the Word of God, and too lazy to witness about the good news of the Gospel, because he's gripped by complacency.

What is thy name? My name is Jealousy. I specialize in keeping this man dissatisfied with what he has and who he is, and I make sure that he's broken up by what other people have. I keep reminding him of the Joneses and how much more they have even though they don't seem to work as hard as he does. He's even jealous of the spiritual gifts of other people. I make sure that he competes for recognition and rewards in areas that he's not even gifted in. And then I compel him to keep scratching and clawing away at these other people so that there will be constant bickering and dissension and divisions in the Body of Christ because no kingdom will ever amount to much when there's jealousy in the house.

What is thy name? My name is Control. This is my twin brother, Manipulation. Together with our cousin Insecurity, we're the product of what is called an inferiority complex. We've convinced this man that other people are actually better than he is. But then we assist him in overcompensating for that by showing him that he can prove himself better than others if he can manipulate and control them. That's where the sense of power comes from. So he spends most of his time working on plots, schemes, and strategic maneuvers to set up traps, to trip people up, and to use them to his own advantage. He's addicted to this kind of life, but he's running out of tricks and running out of friends because of his need to control them.

What is thy name? My name is Pride. My purpose is to keep this man wrapped up in his own importance. So I constantly have to stroke his ego. I won't let him confess to any wrongdoing. I absolutely forbid any feelings of remorse or repentance because that's a sign of weakness. So I have to keep counseling him to think more highly of himself than he ought to think. Already I've got him believing that nobody knows as much as he knows; that nobody's ever done what he's done; that he's the greatest, the best, the first, the most and the only one of his kind. I have to keep the man puffed up so that he remains in bondage to a distorted view of himself. He's never read that pride goeth before destruction.

What is thy name? My name is Religion. I really come as an angel of light. I'm the one who influences this man to hang around the church but for all the wrong reasons. I make sure that he's got on the appropriate apparel, and that he's mastered the appropriate language. He's full of "Hallelujahs" and "Praise the Lords." I helped him to memorize the whole Bible so that he can impress people with his head knowledge of the Word. I make sure that he focuses on only the artificial and superficial aspects of the faith, and that he does just enough to fool some of the people some of the time.

What is thy name? My name is Legion, for we are many. Surely, we can see that there's a storm raging inside of this man. Now, let's go back to verse three so that we can learn even more about the predicament that he faced. First of all, his condition of uncleanness forced him to live in a state of isolation. He was out there among the tombs. To associate with uncleanness might result in defilement of oneself. That's why the man with the unclean spirits was forced to live among other unclean things, like corpses in the town cemetery. And that's what the devil wants to do to the life of every true believer. He wants to keep us separated from the sweet fellowship of God and from the life-producing community of faith. He wants to keep us cut off from the quality of life that our family and friends enjoy. While they're living it up in the city, this man is living it down in the cemetery. They made their plans in the city, while he meandered about with no agenda, no goals for himself. His family and friends were able to eat what they had earned, but this man with the unclean spirits had to forage for scraps and leftovers at the edge of the city limits. He discovered that the quality of life for him diminished day by day because he was destined to live out his life among dead things and dead people. You see, when you have an unclean spirit, everything that you see, everything that you touch, everything that you do reeks of deadness—things that are nonproductive, ineffective, and incapable of giving life.

Gossiping with your neighbor every morning—that's a dead thing. Watching five hours of soap operas and TV talk shows a day—that's a dead thing. Snorting and snuffing and drinking to escape reality—dead things. Sneaking and peeking in all the wrong places, trying to satisfy legitimate needs in illegitimate ways—dead things. Unclean spirits cause us to be isolated from the abundant life that Jesus came to offer, and force us into a state of misery, despair, and desperation—a state where we can never find satisfaction or fulfillment or enjoyment among the dead things of this world. The man was at an all time low because he was living a life of separation.

Another thing that we notice about the condition of the demoniac is that he was totally out of control. No man could bind him. As opposed to the Holy Spirit, who does everything decently and in order, an unholy spirit will have you doing things indecently and out of order. The man lost control of his mind. He had fits of distemper. He was violent and confused, strong-willed and independent. He would not submit to authority. He would not respect the rights of others. He knew no boundaries when it came to possessions. He took whatever he wanted. His lack of restraint hurt other people. His tongue was not tamed. He didn't know when to speak and when to be silent. He exercised no discretion in his mannerisms. He disregarded what was appropriate and what was inappropriate. Reason and common sense escaped him. The man was totally out of control because of these unclean spirits.

Verse five reveals that his self-esteem was slowly deteriorating. He was out there in the mountains and among the tombs, all day and all night (every day and every night), crying out and cutting himself with stones. This is what sin will do to you. And the longer you remain in bondage to sin, the more likely you are to just make yourself sick. You get tired of the same old ruts, the same old habits, the same old lies, the same old stench. But every time you try to pull yourself up and get back on the right track, you fall right back into the same old jealousies, the same old pride, the same old deception, the same old cover-ups. And you don't like yourself very much at all. Your self-esteem drops so low that you begin doing self-destructive things and believing that you'd be better off dead than alive, because to live like this is not living at all.

Now, I don't mean that to be suicidal is a good thing, but the key element here is that consciousness and conviction of sin is a point of spiritual crisis. In fact, it's a pivotal point in our lives. It's a sign that all is not lost. It's an indication that there's still hope for the sin-sick soul. It's a cry for deliverance. Yet God will not deliver anybody from sin against his will. You have to want it badly enough and deeply enough that nothing and nobody else matters. Bring your emptiness to God because the void that we feel can only be filled by the Living Water Himself.

Verse six tells us that the man saw Jesus afar off. And that's when despair turned into hope. When he saw Jesus, a little spark of sunshine ignited his sore, aching feet, and they began leaping toward the Master. This is what God wants all of us to do with our unclean spirits. He wants us to pick up our sin burdens and run to Him with them. We can't clean ourselves up before we come, so we must come as we are. Run to Jesus with your sins and then reverence Him enough to do what the man with the unclean spirits did—bow down in the Master's presence. He began to do things decently and in order now, in verse six. He bowed at the feet of Jesus to worship Him. Anybody who truly desires to be delivered from every yoke of bondage has got to be willing to worship God with a heart and a spirit and an attitude that is acceptable unto God. We can't come into His holy presence pretending that we have no sin. We can't come before the Lord acting as if we deserve any of His blessings. We can't come into worship with our own agenda or by comparing ourselves with other people. God sees every crack and crevice of the human heart, and there is nothing any of us have that would make us look good in the sight of God, except the blood of His Son Jesus. That ought to humble us enough when we come to worship and cause us to cry out "Lord, have mercy on me." This man's heart was right when he worshiped Jesus, and that's why the Lord accepted him. That's why the Lord purged him of all of his uncleanness, because deep down in his heart, the man truly desired to be delivered.

So then, after the storms of our lives are over, we should expect God to act in a mighty way. When the storm comes, know that we serve a God who is always up to something. Expect to see more of His glory. Expect God to take us to a higher level. After the storm is over, expect a new deposit of faith that will prepare us for an even greater dimension of ministry and a deeper level of Christian witness. If we hold out after the storm, deliverance will surely come.

The Judgment Seat Of Christ

1 Corinthians 5:1-10

As another year draws to a close, many of us are inclined to take a year-end inventory of our assets and our liabilities. We somehow need to know that even if we haven't moved forward toward our life's goals, at least we haven't gone backward. And so we spend time reflecting on the successes and failures of another year of living.

Individuals are not the only ones who do this type of year-end evaluation. Many businesses are known to do a yearly personnel assessment, called a performance review. Using a certain criteria that is given to the employee in advance, corporate executives conduct a review of one's performance for the purpose of rankings or promotions, and to reward good performance with merit pay increases.

Even in the educational realm, this is the time of year when semesters draw to a close and student performance is cumulatively evaluated. Therefore, at this time of the year it's not an unusual thing for believers to set our minds on not only the spiritual assessments of the past year, but also on the ultimate evaluation of our life's work and service to God. "For we must all appear before the judgment seat of Christ; that every one may receive the things done in his body, according to that he hath done, whether it be good or bad" (2 Corinthians 5:10).

This comes as no surprise to the student of the Word of God because the entire Bible speaks of a God who will judge the world. His judgment began in the garden of Eden with the rebellion of our first parents. He judged the world by water at the time of Noah. And what about the judgment that fell on Sodom and Gomorrah? The record shows that he not only brought judgment upon the heathen nations but upon His chosen people as well. The justice of God is the foundation of the cross of Jesus Christ. The whole of the Gospel message points to a time of testing by fire. As sure as the earth is round and night follows day, we must all appear before the Judgment Seat of Christ.

It is generally accepted that the Judgment Seat of Christ will take place when Jesus returns to take all believers to be with Him in heaven. In contrast, the Great White Throne Judgment convenes many years later, just before the final phase of eternity. Attendance at one or the other is required of everyone. There can be no exceptions, no special deferment. If a person is unsaved and dies in his sins, he will be judged at the Great White Throne Judgment. If a person is a born-again believer, he will be judged at the Judgment Seat of Christ. At this judgment, the believers' service to God will be reviewed and rewarded. We will be held responsible for our stewardship of life—and that means everything, for God shall bring every work into judgment, with every secret thing, whether it be good or whether it be evil. "For there is nothing covered, that shall not be revealed; neither hid, that shall not be known" (Luke 12:2). "For the time is come that judgment must begin at the house of God: and if it first begin at us, what shall the end be of them that obey not the gospel of God? And if the righteous scarcely be saved, where shall the ungodly and the sinner appear?" (1 Peter 4:17-18).

So then, the two-fold purpose of the Judgment Seat of Christ is to give an account and to receive rewards on the basis of our stewardship. For the Apostle Paul says it is required of a steward that he be found faithful. But found faithful to whom? If we look over into the fourth chapter of his first letter to the Corinthians, we see where the apostle penned these words to the church: "But with me it is a very small thing that I should be judged of you, or of man's judgment" (1 Corinthians 4:3a). John says if our hearts condemn us not, we have confidence before God. But Paul didn't even trust his own heart, his own judgment of himself. His clear conscience did not acquit him before the judicial bench. Paul knew that there is only one judge—and that's the Lord Jesus.

It's so easy to fall into the trap of comparing ourselves to other people: our goodness to their goodness, our ministry to their ministry, our gifts to their gifts, our sins to their sins. In fact, judging others is the quick and easy way to feel good about ourselves. As long as I'm thinking about your weaknesses, then I don't have to deal with my own. The easiest way to justify the mistakes in my house is to find worse ones in my neighbor's house. We look at our brother and then repeat what Peter said about John: Lord, what about him? But Jesus' response to Peter was: What is that to you? You just make sure that you follow me.

Some folk find it hard to follow Jesus or any manifestation of His presence because they're so wrapped up in other people. But if you've ever been there yourself, then you know that in the manifest presence of God, He alone so captures our attention that nothing and nobody else matters to a child of God. God will not share His glory with anybody else. And it's unthinkable that while God is dealing with me, I can focus on Him and you at the same time! Can the hungry accuse the beggar? Can the sick mock the ill? Can the blind judge the deaf? Can one sinner condemn another sinner? What is that to you? There is only one person that is qualified to judge, and that person is neither preaching nor listening to this message.

You see, brothers and sisters, there are two reasons that scripture bears out that disqualify human beings from the role of judge. The first reason is that we just don't know enough. The story is told of an old man who was seen every day by some kids playing in the park. The man came walking up the sidewalk all by himself and didn't stop until he reached the old general store on the corner. After a few minutes, the kids saw him on his return trip with a half-gallon of ice cream in a clear plastic bag. Every day at the same time of the evening, the old man went through his usual routine. Well, the young children came to the conclusion that either this fellow was eating a whole lot of ice cream, or that there were a lot of people at his house who consumed a whole lot of ice cream.

Well, one day the old man, for some reason, sat down on a park bench on his return trip from the store, and the children had a chance to talk with him. "Why do you eat so much ice cream?" they questioned. "Oh, this is not for me," replied the man. "My wife is terminally ill, and it's just the two of us at the house. So I try to take good care of her by cooking her favorite things for dinner each day. She loves to eat two scoops of vanilla ice cream for desert. So after I finish cooking her dinner, I always walk to the store for the vanilla ice cream that she loves so well." "But why do you have to buy it every day?" asked one of the kids. "Oh, we don't have a refrigerator at the house, so there's no way to keep it fresh over night," the man replied. "Then why do you buy so much?" inquired another. "It's the only size that they sell at this store," replied the man. In all of our wisdom, we just don't know enough to hold the gavel in other people's lives.

The second reason that we disqualify as judges is that we're just not good enough. Romans 2:1 says, "Therefore thou art inexcusable, O man, whosoever thou art that judgest: for wherein thou judgest another, thou condemnest thyself; for thou that judgest doest the same things." Well, to whom is Paul addressing such a strong rebuke? It could be anybody who filters God's Word through his own opinions; anybody who dilutes God's mercy with his own preferences. He's the Prodigal Son's elder brother who refused to attend his brother's party. He's the ten-hour worker, upset because the one-hour worker got the same wage as he got. He's the faultfinding brother or sister, obsessed by other people's shortcomings and oblivious to his own: whoever you are, you're just not good enough to call the shots. We don't hold the gavel, God does; and we know that His judgment is right. His judgment is based on the whole truth and nothing but the truth. God takes every detail into consideration. He knows how every single factor plays into any given situation, and He alone has the power to determine outcome. We don't hold the gavel, and that's why we have to wait until the righteous judge convenes an open court. Oh, it's going to be a public trial. The angels will be there, and all the saints of the ages will be looking on. And then will every man receive the praise of God because every man will have to answer to God for himself.

At the Judgment Seat, there will be no place to hide. At the Judgment Seat, we won't be able to plot and scheme and make ourselves look good, for God always sees us just as we are. At the Judgment Seat, it will truly be just Jesus and me. No attorney to represent me, no witnesses to corroborate my testimony. There will be no jury nor deliberation. The ultimate verdict concerning our faithfulness will be His and His alone. And because Jesus is the righteous judge who will judge without respect of persons, we will not have to worry about receiving a fair trial. You see, God has this vast information network. Malachi 3:16 says that God has a book of remembrance. That means that He can download everything we've ever said or done in the twinkling of an eye. And whatever God chooses to reveal, we won't be able to dispute the facts. In our world, men can appeal to a higher court, but there's no higher court in heaven itself than the Judgment Seat of Christ.

Many of us might stand in shame as we see our lives pass before us. Every single detail will be brought into the final verdict, with every motive and action accounted for in its context. In other words, we shall be turned inside out. God has an eternal memory of every word we have spoken since we've been saved. Oh, we won't be ashamed of the good things we've said. But what about our idle words? You know, the gossip, the slander, the criticism, the prejudice. What about the time when somebody upset you and instead of exercising self-control, you just spat out venomous words that you wished you hadn't said? What about the promises you made to people that you never intended to keep? Jesus says in Luke 12:3, "Therefore whatsoever ye have spoken in darkness shall be heard in the light; and that which ye have spoken in the ear in closets shall be proclaimed upon the housetops." But then, what about those times when we should have spoken up about injustices and we chose to keep silent because it was too risky to get involved? What about those unspoken words? It's all about exercising good stewardship of the things in our trust.

Well, what other kinds of things will the Lord be testing by fire at the Judgment Seat? For one thing, He will test the way we have treated other believers. Jesus says, "He that receiveth a prophet in the name of a prophet shall receive a prophet's reward; and he that receiveth a righteous man in the name of a righteous man shall receive a righteous man's reward. And whosoever shall give to drink unto one of these little ones a cup of cold water only in the name of a disciple, verily I say unto you, he shall in no wise lose his reward" (Matthew 10:41-42). We shall be tested on how we exercise our authority over others. The Word says let not many of you become teachers, my brethren, knowing that as such we shall incur a stricter judgment. For those of us who divide the Word of truth, we're charged to study all about it and let the truth go forth. The Lord will judge us on how we used our God-given abilities, our time, our money, as well as our suffering for the sake of His name. "Blessed are ye, when men shall revile you, and persecute you, and shall say all manner of evil against you falsely, for my sake. Rejoice, and be exceeding glad: for great is your reward in heaven" (Matthew 5:11-12a).

Those who master the old nature will receive the incorruptible crown. Those who successfully endure temptations will receive the crown of life. Those who win souls shall reap the crown of rejoicing. The crown of righteousness is promised to those who love the doctrine of the rapture. And to faithful preachers and teachers of the Word shall be given the crown of glory.

But not everybody will be happy. There will be people at the Judgment who will find that so much of what they did was of the flesh and not of God because much of their works will not stand the test of fire. There are a lot of public ministries that are going to go down in flames at the Judgment Seat. The fire is going to take the big showy life of every man and burn it until nothing but a pile of ashes is left. Not only that, but every dime that goes into any ministry will need to be answered for before the Judgment Seat of Christ.

One day God will reveal the true motives behind every deed done in the body. Every false accusation, all cruelty, gossip, and misunderstandings will be cleared up at the Judgment Seat. All the "he-say-she-say" arguments will be silenced. And matters that are still unresolved between us and God and His people will be the subject of review and judgment. Paul tells the Corinthians to "...judge nothing before the time, until the Lord come, who both will bring to light the hidden things of darkness, and will make manifest the counsels of the hearts..." God searches the heart first, then according to our ways and the fruit of our doings, we shall receive our just reward. For behold, He comes with cloud, and every eye shall see him, and his reward is in his hand.

Brothers and sisters, it's just comforting to know that the one who hung on the cross for our sins will be our judge. The friend who sticks closer than a brother will be our judge. The physician who healed our wounds with His own blood, the shepherd who gathered us in his arms and carried us to his bosom, He will be our judge. Jesus will write upon us a new name, and He will confess our name before the Father. But we shall not all have the same privileges; for the way we live now will have an eternal effect upon our spiritual lives. The persons we are today will determine the rewards we receive tomorrow.

Knowing that we must all stand before the judge of the universe and give an account of ourselves is an excellent reason to live out our days in the fear of the Lord. Deeds that have value and survive the examination by fire are those performed in accordance with the Word of God, by faith; in the power of the Holy Spirit, willingly; sincerely; and as unto the Lord and not as unto men. People who strive to be men-pleasers in their service to God already have their reward, but their deeds will account for nothing at the Judgment Seat of Christ. What really matters is that we hear these words from the lips of the Master Himself: "Well done, good and faithful servant."

So then, until the Lord comes back, we should learn to begin each day at the Judgment Seat of Christ. We should humble ourselves before God early in the morning, and try to see ourselves as we really are in the sight of God. Ask Him to shine His light upon our souls.

Allow Him to turn us inside out. Begin each day finding out from God what is displeasing in His sight. Ask for help in being honest about ourselves. Confess our sins before Him, and then turn away from every ungodly pursuit. Begin each day at the Judgment Seat. Ask God to provide you with witnessing opportunities during the day and to allow you to be attuned to the leading of the Holy Spirit. We should begin each day asking God to cleanse us and to teach us how to love one another—to teach us not to abuse our liberties, but to be as generous as we can be. Just plead the blood of Jesus every day at the Judgment Seat of Christ.

Hurt People Hurt People

1 Samuel 30:1-10

Life hurts! Even for Christians. We cannot deny pain or suppress our emotions. We must deal with the reality of every circumstance in life. Many Christians today suffer from broken hearts. Some of us have carried the scars of rejection all of our lives. It could have been physical or sexual abuse, divorce, death, or abandonment. Or maybe it was the pain and disappointment that we experienced when our children did not do so well in life. Although we did the best we knew how, we still ended up living with heavy guilt, shame, and condemnation. And so, we harbor deep hurts and resentments and frustrations.

Well, one of the first things that we have to accept about life is that there are some wounds that won't heal overnight. Even in the course of nature, you have to apply the remedy and then let time take its course. And we've got to accept the fact that you can't neglect any part of the treatment along the way or else you might end up with an infection developing in the wound. You know, that's the way it is with our emotions. Wounds, rejection, abuse, broken hearts. But a brokenhearted person can easily get out of control. And if the pain is not properly and permanently dealt with, then we're likely to find hurting people, hurting other people.

In this scripture passage, King David and his men were returning home from battle. When they entered into their village, they were shocked to discover that it was destroyed by fire. Then they learned that the Amalekites took their wives and children away as hostages. What a tragedy! What an affliction to discover that everything you have is gone, that everybody that you love is gone, and that you may never see them alive again. Scripture says that the men were overcome with both grief and anger. We cannot deny that the pain here is real. Their grief was surely justified. These men were experiencing the depths of human despair. The loss was too great; it was extreme, heinous, and horrendous. And we find them doing what any one of us would do in a similar situation: they wept aloud until they had no strength left to weep.

We've got to understand today that it's not a shame for men to cry. We're looking here at a whole army of men crying without restraint. Truly there are some situations and some circumstances in life where it would be a sin not to cry. Tears are an indication to us that our God is sensitive to and understanding of the human predicament. Our tears spring out of a built-in overflow valve that kicks in when words are just too inadequate to express our deepest emotions. So the shedding of tears is a sign of a healthy condition of the soul. Only a mean-hearted person would refuse to shed tears. It's an important step in the process of grief recovery. Tears are not the end; they're only the beginning of inner healing.

And so, David and his men sat down and had themselves a good cry. But we've got to be careful that we don't go too far and allow ourselves to get caught up in a pity party. You see, it's all right to cry, but we've got to know when enough is enough. Tears can be beneficial, but only for a season. When we continue to wallow in our own tears, we end up aborting the process of healing. Tears serve the purpose of transporting us from a state of emotional upheaval to a state of rational thinking. But after the tears are gone, reason and intellect should return so that we're able to move on and move up out of our state of despair.

That's the problem that so many of us have today. We get hung up in our pain. We become immobilized by our grief. We fail to apply the proper remedy to our wounds, and that's why they never heal. You may not be able to see it on the outside, but many people today are still bearing scars and wounds from their past. And you can tell that the healing is not complete because somebody may unknowingly and inadvertently touch these sensitive areas and spark an unexpected reaction.

That's why, as members of the Body of Christ, we need to be careful how we speak to and act toward other people. We need a discerning spirit that will enable us to look beyond surface things and to determine the spiritual condition of our sisters and brothers. This is every believer's responsibility. We actually miss out on so many opportunities to minister to hurting people because we're content to tread in the shallow waters of chitchat, platitudes, and politeness. Superficial, artificial relationships are found in so many of our churches because we fail to make spirit-to-spirit contact with those whom we see and interact with on a regular basis.

That's why there can be no true fellowship among believers. People are reluctant to share their pain, unless they are convinced that we really care about how they feel. Most folk would rather bottle up their feelings inside than to be the hot topic of everybody's conversation. It's a sad commentary on the Church that we shoot our wounded. The Church is supposed to be a hospital for the sick, not an institution where everybody pretends to be well and to have no need of the Great Physician. The truth is that all of us are sick, and none of us have the power to heal ourselves. We have to give all of our broken pieces to the Master Healer, for He alone can make us whole. That's what Christianity is all about. It's not about our individual performance on a test. Christianity is about people—the hurting, the lame, the blind, the crippled, the broken-hearted—being led into the presence of Jesus so that they can be made whole again. People who have allowed God to deal with their hurts and pains are in a much better position to show empathy and compassion toward others, because they're careful not to hurt.

Well, let's look at what happens to David's men, when they fail to move on in the healing process. David was in the same boat his men were in. His property was burned. His two wives were taken captive by the enemy as well. He cried his heart out right along with the others. But quite unexpectedly his men re-directed their hatred away from the Amalekites and began to pour all of their swelled emotions and rage onto David. Everybody in the pity party was convinced that David was to blame for all of their troubles. So they started a mutiny. Their emotions clouded the reality of just who the real enemy was. In an unhealthy emotional state, there's a need to strike out at somebody. And if we find it impossible to hurt the ones who have hurt us, then the next best thing will be sufficient.

This is what is commonly known as transference. When sorrow and pain from the past have not been resolved or healed through the process of forgiveness, the soul seeks out another sin bearer or scapegoat, in an attempt to mete out justice in his or her own way. The likelihood of this type of projection occurring is more common than one might think. At any given time, any one of us may find ourselves either on the giving or receiving end of a transference. Most times, because we are unaware of the real problem and because we are unsuspecting in our relationships with people, we tend to misjudge and misconstrue negative and inappropriate behaviors. Also, our own reactions serve to complicate matters even further. Before we know it, discontent and divisiveness have occurred in our families, on our jobs, and even in the Body of Christ. People begin to turn against each other, forgetting who the real enemy is. If we don't deal properly and promptly with our hurts and pains, they will fester and we stand in danger of becoming calloused and bitter and weak and ineffective in our individual and our corporate lives.

Well, sometimes God will allow His servants to face insurmountable odds, to be overcome with pain or grief. Sometimes He will allow circumstances to go beyond our control so that we can be reminded that God still sits upon His throne. And that's good news to anybody who has ever struggled with personal failure, emotional scars from the past, or weaknesses of the flesh in the present. The good news is that we have a High Priest who understands frustration, anxiety, feelings of isolation and abandonment. He knows what it is to cry out in agonizing pain. He understands how people can hurt you and turn against you. He understands how people who refuse to be healed can spread their contagious diseases. He knows. He understands. That's why we can come boldly to the throne of grace where we can transfer all of our burdens to Him.

Spiritual Ups And Downs

1 Kings 19:1-18

In some evangelical circles today, you will find Christians who are of the conviction that true believers are always up and never down. In fact, they will condemn you and correct you and judge you and instruct you on how Christians must always show themselves to others in only the finest light. These well-meaning folk firmly believe that all of us should be baptized in the Holy Ghost with the evidence of a smiling face. But the Bible portrays a realistic view of what we can expect from this Christian life, and from the looks of things biblically, the downs are just as much a part of our spiritual growth process as the ups. So even the greatest of the saints of God are revealed to us in the Bible as sometimes up and sometimes down.

My Bible tells me that Job was a perfect and upright man, but he still found himself battling with situations that were difficult both to deal with and to explain. The prophet Jonah was used by God to effect one of the greatest revivals of all time. And yet, it was just after this great spiritual high that Jonah sank into an all-time spiritual low. David was the greatest warrior and the greatest king that Israel had ever known, but his own moral failure plummeted him to pillows wet with tears. Even Paul was not exempt from low moments. Study the lives of all the great saints and you will discover a cycle of ups and downs, ups and downs.

Our scripture passage puts us right in the middle of the cycle—right where the pendulum begins to swing in the life and ministry of one of the greatest prophets that ever lived. We don't even know where Elijah came from; his appearance is just as mysterious as his disappearance. But he was God's man of the hour, and he was a man of God. We see him at the brook Cherith as a man totally dependent upon God. We see him at Zarephath where God sustains him by the multiplication of flour and oil in a widow's house. We see how he miraculously brings her son back to life. We see Elijah being used mightily by God because he has learned to be obedient unto the Lord. He knew how to conduct himself in the public arena. He knew how to live for God in the deserts. He was a man prepared—he was prepared for the showdown at Mount Carmel, where he stood alone against the indifferences of God's people. He stood alone against the anger of eight hundred and fifty prophets of Baal and against all the royal court of the king. This was Elijah, who slaughtered those evil prophets and who brought the fear of God into the heart of a wicked king when the rains came down. We read in the last verse of Chapter Eighteen that the hand of God was upon Elijah and he became a marathon runner. He ran from the top of Mount Carmel to Jezreel (outrunning King Ahab, who rode in the finest chariot of his day). How was he able to run eighteen to twenty miles in a thunderstorm? The hand of God was upon him.

And yet we see this man of God in the opening verses of Chapter Nineteen as a totally different person—weak, faithless, and scared. We can't pass up the opportunity to strike a note of warning here. There's always danger in victory. Beware of moments of great exaltation. Beware of reaching life's goals. There's something about paying off the house—about owning the car. There's something mystical about getting that well-earned promotion, about obtaining that degree, or getting that last child out of school. In those high moments of victory or success or accomplishment—when you're sitting up high—it's so easy to be brought down low by the enemy. He shows up with his weapons, his lies, his deception, his temptations, and he lays the first snare for his victims; that is, to get us to look at our circumstances instead of looking at God.

This was Elijah's first mistake. After King Ahab reported to his wicked wife Jezebel the victory at Mount Carmel and the deaths of all of the prophets of Baal by the hand of Elijah, Jezebel was provoked to utter a threat to Elijah's life. She swore by the very gods who had been helpless to save the prophets, that Elijah himself would be dead within twenty-four hours. And the record says that when Elijah found out, he became afraid and ran for his life. But in light of the fact that he had seen what God had done to the prophets of Baal and had witnessed fire come down from heaven when he prayed, why would this servant of the Lord be so afraid of evil words from an evil woman? Because in the condition that he found himself in, and looking at the circumstances through the eyes of the flesh, Elijah knew that Jezebel had the means and the power to do just what she had sworn by her gods to do, so he ran for his life.

Sisters and brothers, we have to understand that whenever we come out of a spiritual high without making the effort to refuel and to regroup—whenever we allow ourselves to become spiritually depleted—we're more likely to react to our circumstances in an abnormal way. Our minds can trick us and cause us to blow things out of proportion. When we forget to study God's Word and become slack in our prayer life, before we know it we'll begin to do things totally out of character and unbecoming for a child of God. And Satan is happy, because it means that we have taken our eyes off God and His spiritual revelations. If Elijah had not been in a weakened condition (because of his great spiritual victory), he would have declared before Jezebel what Isaiah describes as the inheritance of the servants of the Most High God: No weapon formed against me shall prosper and that every tongue that rises against me in judgment shall be found false. That's our inheritance, and it doesn't mean that the weapons won't form up against us, it just means that they won't prosper. They won't succeed in wiping us out and destroying us and rendering us ineffective in doing the Lord's work. But the prophet, at that point, was not where he ought to have been spiritually, so he took his first step downward on the road to despondency and despair.

Verse four says that when he got to Beersheba, he left his servant there. Now, Beersheba is about a one hundred twenty-mile journey from Jezreel. So by this time Elijah had pushed himself to the point of physical exhaustion. He was already spiritually empty. Now tired and hungry, he made another bad decision. He set himself up for Satan's second attack by leaving his servant there and inviting loneliness to set in. The devil can do his greatest work on us when he finds us all alone. He presented the ultimate temptation to Eve when she was alone—away from her husband. He tried it again with Jesus when He, too, was alone in the wilderness. Peter denied his Lord when he was all alone. There was nobody to give him godly counsel, nobody to touch and agree with him in prayer, nobody to talk to or to share the deepest concerns of his heart. No encouragement, no edification, no objectivity. Being alone can sometimes work against us mentally and emotionally. Everybody needs somebody sometime. God created us for fellowship with one another. After all the good that God had created, with all of the beauty and excellence of the natural world, when God created man, He Himself declared that it was not good for man to be alone. So He made a helpmeet for him. God's plan for the prosperity of man's soul is that we should live in close community; that there should be a spiritual partnership among believers based upon the knowledge of truth, a common goal; and that we should exhibit unconditional love one for the other, so that we can be sustained through both the ups and the downs of life. It is not good that man should be alone.

But Elijah seemed to have ignored the warning signs of depression and plunged into that great and foreboding path of wilderness existence. He bottomed out in verse four, as he sat under a broom tree, sizing up the whole of his life and ministry. From the pit of despair he cried out, "It is enough now, O Lord." In other words, I've had it. I can't cope with this thing any longer. I'm at my wit's end. I'm ready to throw in the towel. It's better for me to die than to live like this.

Here was a man of God who had just had a mountaintop experience; one who had been a powerful instrument in the hands of God; somebody who took a bold stand for God. Through him many mighty and miraculous advances were made for the Kingdom, and yet we find that not even he was exempt from the feelings of frustration and failure and uselessness and disappointments that life has to offer in this world. James says of Elijah that he was a man of like passions just as we are. So it's not an uncommon thing for believers to become discouraged in life. It's not uncommon for the saints of God to be found gripped by feelings of inadequacy, defeat, and lack of purpose. Many of us today can find something in the details of this story that we can relate to. Some of us can say "been there, done that" about Elijah's despondency. But we know that he has bottomed out here because he said he was ready to give up the ghost and go the way of all men. That's what he said, but that's not what he meant. You see, his cry for death was really a cry for help. If Elijah had really wanted to die, Jezebel would have been happy to oblige him. He didn't have to run so fast and so far. But then most people who have bottomed out, who are physically and emotionally and spiritually empty, are simply lost in their own "lostness." They're not ready to give in and to give up on life. They just want to be rescued. They want somebody to give them the solution to their problems. What they crave is a helping hand and a merciful heart.

Most desperate people would jump at the chance of finding a way out of their troubles and fulfilling their dreams. But sometimes God has to allow us to follow the dictates of our own wills until we get to the point of desperation so that we can realize our own deficiencies, our own sense of pride and self-righteousness. Then and only then are we in a right position for God to elevate us to the next spiritual level. Somebody has said that the way up is down. The Bible says, he that humbles himself shall be exalted. God is waiting for some of us to just bottom out so that He can step into our situations and glorify Himself.

Let's look at His divine intervention in verse five. And as we do, we discover how very practical the Lord is in ministering to His servants when they're down. First of all, we find Elijah asleep, and an angel of the Lord awakens him with a nutritious meal. Very basic and very practical. How often do we get so caught up in doing things for God, in caring for our families, in meeting the demands of our careers that we fail to give our bodies a much-needed rest and a proper diet? We seem to take for granted the restorative powers of good sleep and good food. But in order to be at our best spiritually, we have to be at our best physically. God created us, and He has provided what the body needs for optimum production. God holds us accountable for good stewardship of our physical temples. We can't neglect our physical needs and expect to have strong minds and quickened spirits. God has made provisions for body, soul, and spirit. So the first step that God takes in lifting

Elijah up out of his state of despair is to minister to the needs of his body.

The second step is to take care of his spiritual needs. When we're down in our spirits, what we need is to go back to our spiritual roots. In other words, go to church. That's where Elijah was going in verse eight. Mount Horeb is the mount of God. This is the place where Moses encountered God, where he received his commission. Horeb is the place where He brought water out of a rock and where the people stripped off their ornaments in token of repentance. Horeb symbolizes the sacredness of God's dealings with man's sins. It's a spiritual reminder of God's providential care for His people. Whenever we allow ourselves to sink into the pit of despondency and despair, the road to recovery ought to lead us to a divine encounter with our God, and it ought to increase our spiritual awareness of Him and Who He really is. We have to come to realize, when we're down, that in order to move up, we have to first look up unto the hills. That's where our help comes from. It's only when we look up that we can find the strength to get up, the will to stand up, the courage to speak up, and then the determination to stay up. We must take that journey back to our spiritual roots. And we have to go there with a holy expectation. Expect God to be faithful to His Word. Expect God to manifest His glory there. Expect to hear a word of direction from the Lord.

Elijah was on his way up now as he journeyed toward the mount of God. When he got there, in verse nine, he settled himself down in a cave and heard the voice of God saying: What are you doing here, Elijah? What is my servant doing in a cave? What are you afraid of? What are you guilty of? What is it that you're hiding from? Sometimes it's hard to tell when the servants of God are dwelling in caves. We wear our smiles, we laugh, we play the games, but many of us are cave-dwellers. Our fears and loneliness, frustrations and disappointments have driven us into a cave-like existence. We've lost our dignity, our self-respect, or we're just plain tired of the harshness of life and the phoniness of people. So we come out of our caves just enough to be cordial and polite and respectable, not willing to really reveal our true selves. "What are you doing here, Elijah?"

Alas, now the prophet had an opportunity to speak to his God from the bottom of his heart: "I have been jealous for you, God. My zeal has been great. I have done this and I've done that. I've worked so hard for so long, but what has it all amounted to? I'm a failure. I've made no real difference in anybody's life. Nothing's changed. Nobody will give me any support. They have all deserted you, Lord. I'm all by myself now. And they seek my life to take it away."

It's an honest confession, but really Elijah is being very selfish here. The man is focusing on himself and his accomplishments. He's wallowing in self-pity and self-righteousness. What he's really saying is, "Lord, the problem is not me, it's the other folk." What he's really feeling is that things would be much better if everybody else would just be like me. Elijah doesn't see his fault here, but God does. And yet God does not chide or rebuke him for his honesty. He looks beyond the man's faults and deals with him according to his need. And what Elijah needs most right now is to experience God in a way that he has never experienced Him before. He needs a glimpse of God's glory. He needs the security of God's unchanging love. Elijah needs his sins forgiven. He needs to have his joy restored. He needs a touch of divine favor. Inspite of all of our imperfections, it's comforting to know that when we're down, God knows just what we need when we need it.

That's why the Lord took Elijah up to higher ground—moved him up the spiritual side of the mountain. It's the same opportunity that had been afforded to Moses. For we know that no man can look upon God and live. But every now and then we can be privileged to experience Him just passing by. We need to experience God as we have never experienced Him before. Some of us need a spiritual lift—something or somebody that'll pick us up, turn us around, and point us in the right direction. We need to sense the weight of God's glory resting upon us and, to hear a word from the Lord.

There's a lesson to be learned from Elijah's experience here. You see, when he got to church, in verse eleven, and went on up the spiritual side of the mountain, he heard the sound of a mighty rushing wind that ripped the mountain apart and broke the rocks into pieces. But the scripture says that God was not in the wind. After that the earth began to tremble, and the shaking and rattling of the elements caused a mighty stir on the mountain. But God was not in the earthquake. Then we're told that a great fire appeared. God had answered Elijah's prayer by fire. He had arrested the attention of Moses by fire. Not only that, but we know that our God is a consuming fire. But God was not in the fire. Sometimes we can be guilty of looking for God in all the wrong places. It's significant to us that God was not in the fanfare. God was not in the hoopla. God was not in all of the noise and commotion. God was not in the heat of passion and emotion. He uses these methods sometimes just to get our attention. But the scripture says after the fire there was a ... hush ... hush ... a still, small voice. Hush, hush, somebody's calling your name. (And what I like about the Lord is that He knows His servants by name....) He then asks Elijah: "What are you doing in that cave?

"I know how you're feeling right not, but you let Me decide when enough is enough. Only I know the plans that I have for you. I'm not through with you yet. There is still more work for you to do. I tell you what, go on over to Damascus. And when you get there, I need you to anoint two kings for Me. And when you finish with that, there's a young prophet that needs to be trained. Anoint him to take your place in ministry. And another thing: Who told you that you were in this thing all by yourself? Look around you, Elijah. I've still got seven thousand who have not bowed down to Baal. I've got seven thousand warriors who won't flinch in the face of evil. Look around you, Elijah. I've got me seven thousand soldiers who are ready to move out at my command—seven thousand servants who will never compromise My Name. So you're in good company, Elijah. Cheer up." God will never leave Himself without a witness. And God will never call us to do something for Him and then forsake us just when we need Him the most.

Yes, in this life there will be ups and there will surely be some downs. But the good news is that believers don't have to stay down. Stop looking at your circumstances, and keep your eyes on the God of your circumstances. Take care of your physical and spiritual needs. Go on up to the holy mount of God, and then allow God to reinterpret the situation for you. Let Him clarify your misunderstandings. Let Him re-establish your purpose in life. Let Him provide you with godly companionship—people who will be there to encourage you along the way; people who will help you to get back on your feet again and to get back into the race, so that you can rise to the occasion of your next assignment from God.

Thank God that Elijah didn't stay down long. He continued to be useful to God. In II Kings 2:11, we find that one day, while Elijah was walking and talking with his godly companion, there appeared a chariot of fire and horses of fire, and Elijah just went on up by a whirlwind into the heavens. "They that wait upon the Lord shall renew their strength; they shall mount up (like Elijah) with wings as eagles" (Isaiah 40:31a). I don't know about you, but I've had my ups and I've had my downs in life. Sometimes rising and sometimes falling. But I'm holding on to my faith because some glad morning, when this life is over, I'm gonna spread my wings.

Mercy In The House

John 5:1-9

In this text we see that Jesus was attending a feast in Jerusalem. It's not known for certain which feast it was. It could have been the feast of the Passover, the Tabernacles, or perhaps the feast of Pentecost. In any case, there is a crowd of folk coming into the city busily engaged in the preparations necessary to celebrate this upcoming event.

Now, there was at Jerusalem by the sheep market a pool, which is called in the Hebrew tongue Bethesda. Two possible meanings have been given for the name Bethesda, but the one I like better is "house of mercy." Mercy has been defined as withholding from a person a consequence or a punishment that he truly deserves. It's a showing of kindness or compassion to those who are needy, distressed, or suffering in mind, body, or spirit without regard for pointing out faults and failures. Mercy is not concerned with nit-picking and criticism. Mercy seeks the highest good for the person in distress. So then, Bethesda symbolizes the kind of place that the Church of God ought to be today. We need to come to the understanding that people who are burdened with any kind of infirmity should be able to make their way to the "house of mercy." And when they get there, there ought to be some compassion in the house. There ought to be some healing in the house. There ought to be some affection in the house of mercy. Churches today ought to be full of people who have found mercy for themselves and who are therefore willing to bestow upon others what they themselves have received. Is there any mercy in the house?

The setting in the text is a public place, where many worshippers were engaged in the buying and selling of sheep that may have been used in the required temple sacrifices or in the menus described in the keeping of the feast. And this pool was located in close proximity to the sheep market, a convenient provision of water for the animals to drink. The five porticos, or porches, provide a convenient rest area for the comfort of the people, especially for the multitude of folk who have been drawn to the poolside in anticipation of a great healing miracle.

This crowd is referred to in verse three as a multitude of impotent folk—those who cannot see, those who are not able to walk, and those who are withered, deformed, and paralyzed. They're called impotent because they have lost their productiveness; their capacity for strength and power has been greatly diminished. Impotent describes any condition that hinders one's effectiveness, that mars God's perfect design for what He has created. The text is not confined to just our physical impairments; this crowd of impotent folk represents a broad spectrum of sickness and disease in the world today. They symbolize not only the physically sick, but they also remind us of the mentally and spiritually diseased. You see, sin is a sickening agent that cripples and distorts and paralyzes the human spirit. Sin weakens us, it obstructs our vision, it arrests our spiritual growth, and it leaves us in a state of hopelessness and helplessness that defies treatment and remedy offered by any manmade prescription.

All of us are sick. Because of the fall of Adam in the Garden of Eden, every one of us has been touched by the hand of sin. We have given in to the temptations of the flesh and have been overcome by the symptoms of guilt and shame, doubt and insecurity, low self-esteem, jealousy, strife, and contention. So all of us are sick, and it's all because of sin. Maybe we can see ourselves couched around this pool of Bethesda, waiting for the troubling of the water, waiting for deliverance, waiting for our change to come.

Well, that's the setting of this story. But before we move on to the plot, we've got to focus our attention upon this pool for just a minute because, you see, there are some questions concerning the authenticity of the divine powers that have been attributed to the pool. According to the legend of the time, God gave His angels charge to go down at a certain season and to infuse the water with special but limited healing powers—such that the first person to make contact with the water after it was stirred up would be able to receive the divine blessing of healing. This was what the people believed about the pool of Bethesda. And this was the report that had been passed down over the years. No doubt, there had been some evidences of healing that had taken place just as the legend had declared. But one has to ask himself, Why would God have been so stingy with His mercy, to extend it to only one person, and then to do it on a competitive basis, when we know that God is rich in mercy and that His mercy endureth forever? But the other side of the coin is that there was a subterranean spring underneath the pool that produced periodic pockets of air, causing the pool to bubble up from time to time. Assuming that there were minerals in this water, the effects of moving water far outweigh the effects of stagnant water. Only when the water was disturbed and began to move were the people better able to receive the water's medicinal properties.

But you know that people who have been sick for a long time are not at all interested in geological reports.

They're not likely to be found reading the latest medical journals before they embark upon a treatment plan. How many of us have ever been sick? I mean really sick? And how many times have we found ourselves being able to put aside excruciating pain long enough to read the fine print on the sides of our medicine bottles, to determine the ingredients that went into the product? We'd be surprised to learn that a whole lot of what we take for relief of our own symptoms have barbiturate and amphetamine bases and are likely to be laced with up to eighteen percent alcohol.

The point is that when you're sick and you've been suffering for a long time, and when you've been hurting badly enough, you just keep reaching out in hope that something will somehow bring you some kind of relief. These sick people were desperate for a cure; they had tried everything else and everybody else. All they wanted to know was that they had a shot at deliverance, even if it was a long shot. So they made their way to the "house of mercy," willing to take a gamble on a better life, because to live like that was not really living at all.

We shouldn't be too hard on these wishful thinkers who populated the pool in Jesus' day. We, too, have our myths and legends that we firmly believe will help us and heal us and make us well enough to cope with life and its many problems. Some of us are sold out on astrology and won't make a move or a decision before consulting our daily horoscopes. We've got to know if the moon is in the seventh house and if Jupiter is aligned with Mars. Some of us won't go anywhere without our good luck charms in our pockets. We go to "oil-slinging conventions." Palm readers are making wholesome money from the religious communities today. Some of us are willing to try almost anything that might give us a quick fix or a better grip on what ails us most deep down in our hearts. All of us, in one way or another, can be counted among the crowd of impotent folk at the pool of Bethesda.

Verse five tells us that a certain man was there who, more than any of the other invalids, attracted the attention of the Lord Jesus. Scripture doesn't say why, but it was possible that this particular man was different from all the others. It could have been the severity of the man's physical condition. It might have been the extremity of the man's mental condition. And we do know that man's extremity is always God's opportunity. Perhaps it was the hopelessness of this man's spiritual condition. Very likely the reason was all of the above coupled with the fact that others had family and friends to assist them, but this man was all alone, and that reduced his chances of getting into the pool to just about nil. The Lord Jesus was moved with compassion, for He has always been a friend to the friendless. Maybe that's why He was attracted to this man. To be plagued with the same malady for thirty-eight years is a case of extremity—a case of extreme suffering for an extremely long time. For anybody who suffers from a sickness or disease, thirty-eight years is a long time. To be crippled by ignorance or to be in bondage to prejudice and persecution, thirty-eight years is a long time. To be afflicted by injustices, to have your potential snuffed out by hostility and to be oppressed by evildoers, thirty-eight years is a long, long time. That's long enough for faith to fade and for hope to die out. And so, Jesus was moved with compassion.

Verse six tells us something very important about the Lord Jesus. There are two distinct verbs here that sum up the eternal scope of mental and spiritual activity that took place on the inside of Jesus, before He ever spoke a word to the impotent man. The verse says that He saw and that He knew. That ought to be comforting news to every believing heart—the fact that the Lord sees what nobody else can see. The periphery of His vision is from everlasting to everlasting. He sees the end from the beginning. His foresight is just as reliable as His hindsight. When Jesus looks upon our condition and our circumstances, thank God that He's able to see things as they really are. He sees every contributing factor. He sees every potential and every possibility in us. He sees every obstacle and every struggle. Whenever Jesus looks upon a man, He sees every sincere desire in his heart. He sees every point of discouragement. The Lord sees the hurt and the pain. He sees the wounds and the scars. He sees both the tears and the blood that have been shed in trying to reach our goals, to fulfill our dreams, and to be all that God created us to be. Jesus sees our need to be delivered.

Whatever He sees, He fully understands. The Lord sees AND He knows. He knows what it's like to be lonely. He knows what it takes to turn things around. He knows how much we have given of ourselves. He knows why we do what we do. Jesus knows how many prayers we have prayed. He knows how hard it is to hold on when your strength is constantly giving out. The Lord knows how difficult it is to hold your head up in the face of criticism and condemnation. He knows what it's like to be broken and shattered on the inside because the condition you're in is more despicable to you than it is to other people. Thank God that we have a Savior who knows all about it.

Now we're approaching the climax of the story as Jesus poses a potent question to an impotent man: "Do you want to be made whole?" Is it your heart's desire to be set free? Are you sure that you're ready to cut loose from your ineffective and nonproductive life? Or have you grown so accustomed to your handicap that you have simply resigned yourself to the fact that you'll never make it in this world—that nothing can be done to turn things around? Brothers and sisters, "Do you want to be made whole?" is more than a question. It's a probe and a prompting for the man at the pool to do a thorough self-examination. And it's a moment of truth that we all must come to. It's a point of spiritual crisis that's pivotal to our progress in the Kingdom. Are we satisfied with who we are and with what we know and have of God? Are we content to just wobble along, dragging our feet behind us and giving the appearance of doing the best we can? Do we truly hunger and thirst for the fullness of the abundant life that only Jesus can offer? Do we want to be made whole? What excuses do we have to offer? What crutches do we rest upon? The man in the text said, "Sir, I have no man, when the water is troubled, to put me into the pool." Could it be that we have not because we ask not? Could it be that our own bitterness and self-pity have interfered with our personal relationships, to the extent that we know we need help but our pride just gets in the way? Is it always somebody else's fault that we don't do any better than we do? Are we so afraid of failure and criticism that we would rather stay on a mat that invites pity and sympathy from other people, because that's a much safer place to be? Do you want to be made whole?

Notice that our Lord and Master doesn't have to wait for the man to give a verbal response. He already knew what was in the man. And He knew that this man's heart was now in the right condition for God to be glorified. Sometimes "heart trouble" disqualifies a lot of us from receiving God's choicest blessings. No matter how much and how long we pray for something, God will not grant it because when He searches out the deep crevices of our hearts, He discovers that if He were to grant us our petition, we would end up taking the credit for it ourselves. Or, He might find that after receiving this blessing, we would still not be any more faithful, sacrificial, or obedient to Him. But deep down in the man's heart Jesus saw a willingness to be set free from every yoke of bondage. He saw the brokenness of the outer man that would allow the full release of all selfish desires. He saw a willingness to give God the glory. Whenever man is willing, God is truly able; and we know that God is able even without our willingness. The point is that in order for there to be a breakthrough—in order for a miracle to take place in our lives—we have to connect our faith to God's abilities. We have to cooperate with God. We have to participate in our own deliverance or else Jesus will just walk away and leave us lying upon our beds of unbelief.

God is able to do exceeding abundantly above all that we can ask or think, but it's according to the power of faith that worketh in us. Our faith, then, is the power that causes us to rise up in spite of our predicaments. Faith is the catalyst that elevates us to a level of victory in Jesus. Faith activates the life flow and the energy to put things into motion. Faith wakes up the dead marrow in our bones. Faith is what unites muscles to tendons and tendons to ligaments. Jesus says, "By your faith, rise up. Don't worry about what others may say, rise up. Take your mind off what you don't have; just make use of what you do have. Rise up. All things are possible to them that believe. So rise up. And then take up the responsibility that's yours: take up your bed. Get rid of all excuses, and then walk on off into the newness of life. Walk on into your dreams. Walk on over to your full potential. Walk on past your uncertainties. Walk all over your enemies. Just walk on up the King's highway. Walk on by faith. You can make it. You can do it. You have what it takes. You are more than a conqueror. Wholeness can be yours today. Trust me. Trust me. There's mercy in the house."

A Reason To Rejoice

Luke 10:17-20

In this day of emotionalism, we as Christians can become guilty of allowing a spirit of competition to get us off track. We're tempted to shift our focus from what God has done for us to what it is that we're able to do for God. And the spirit of pride enters in and says, "Look at you, aren't you wonderful!" There is nothing that any of us have that we did not receive from God. The Holy Spirit gives to each of us severally, as He wills to give. Therefore, there's absolutely no place for spiritual pride when we're doing Kingdom work. That's a very basic lesson that Jesus teaches His disciples early on in their ministry. We have to cultivate a spirit of discernment concerning spiritual matters so that we know how to put first things first and know what kind of things really matter the most to God.

On this occasion in our scripture passage, we find that Jesus sent out a group of His disciples with pretty much the same instructions that He gave to the twelve apostles. Notice that He sent them out two by two. That's significant to us because Jesus Himself knew that His servants needed the support of one another. We can't do this thing alone. Every one of us who sets out to do the Lord's bidding ought to have at least one spiritual partner—somebody to be accountable to; somebody to undergird us in prayer and the Word of God; somebody to shoulder the load. Every child of God who is on a mission for the Lord, needs the encouragement and godly counsel of another believer who is also on the same mission, has the same agenda, and who is up against the same opposition. But most of all, they need somebody who trusts in the same God.

Jesus intends for this is to be a shared ministry. There's no place for individual stardom in the Kingdom. God doesn't mean for any of us to try to pull this thing off by ourselves, lest we become puffed up with pride and are tempted to take credit for what rightfully belongs to God. But even more than that, He wants there to be unity within the Body of Christ. For where there is unity, there is strength. The Bible says that one can chase a thousand, but two can put ten thousand to flight. Wherever two or three are gathered in His name, touching and agreeing upon the same thing, He said, "I'll be a God in the midst." And that's why Jesus didn't send His disciples out alone.

He told them that their mission would not be an easy one. There would undoubtedly be many dangers, toils, and snares. They would be as lambs among wolves. And He informed them that they were not to bless the unwilling. Don't try to force the Gospel on those who are unwilling to receive it. We've got to know when it's time to shake the dust from our feet. In other words, the Lord doesn't want us wasting precious time with unnecessary things or people. He told His disciples not to engage in idle conversations. That would be a waste of valuable time. And the people who talk about vain and useless things are not the people that you need to be around. The crowd that's talking about the daily soap operas—that's not your crowd. The people who get caught up in the latest fashions and the newest fads—that's not your crowd. The people who are grumbling, complaining, and gossiping—that's not your crowd. But rather, Jesus instructs His disciples to live in simplicity, heal the sick, and proclaim the Kingdom of God.

And so, the disciples went out as they had been commissioned. As they went about their ministry, they experienced pretty much the same things that we do when we're doing the Lord's work. Some of their hearers responded positively, and others didn't. Some people rejoiced at their message, but some didn't. Many people got healed, but others didn't. Some accepted salvation, but some didn't. And yet they returned to Jesus filled with joy. They were happy to give their praise report to the Lord. *Today's English Version* records them as saying, "Lord, even the demons obeyed us when we commanded them in your name."

There are still some people who have accepted the Lord as their Savior, have been baptized, and have been serving in the church for a long time. They might even have held some pretty high positions in the church, but they seem oblivious to the fact that there's a war going on. We've got to know that we're out here on the battlefield. As the Apostle Paul says, there's a law in my members that wars against the law in my mind and every time I attempt to do good, evil is on every hand. He also tells us that this battle has nothing to do with flesh and blood. We're up against principalities, against powers, against the rulers of the darkness of this world. We're up against spiritual wickedness in high places (see Ephesians 6:12). The enemy's purpose is to take us captive and seduce us away from God, and he'll use any and everything; any and everybody to entrap us, provoke us, and set us up to do things that are against God's will. If he can, he wants to steal our joy, take away our fire and zeal, and make us settle down into a state of complacency and total ineffectiveness. Demon spirits are all around us trying to defeat us on every hand. But the disciples were excited to learn that the name of Jesus has so much power that even the demons obeyed them at the mentioning of that name.

So they returned to Jesus with joy. Their hearts were filled with gladness. Notice that they were not reveling in how much they had done for the Lord. They weren't even complaining about how taxing and tiring the work had been. They didn't even report on how strong the opposition was. Instead, they were all filled with joy over the phenomenal power of the name of Jesus. For there's no other name given among men whereby we might be saved. They knew that the power to do the work did not come from themselves. For this was an unusual kind of power. The power of Jesus' name gave them the ability to get results.

And that's a good definition of power—the ability to get results; to effect some kind of change. Paul told the church at Corinth that the whole idea of the Kingdom of God is wrapped up in this one thing: The kingdom of God is not in word, but in power. Now, in the Greek the word translated for power is "duonimos," which means the same as dynamite. This is the same power that raised Jesus from the dead. And that's the power that we have as believers today. What we have is resurrection power. That's the kind of power that penetrates. It cuts right through a whole lot of stuff. This power cuts through hatred and bitterness; it breaks up stones of opposition; it tears down walls of separation. It's like "Roto Rooter": It gets into places in our spirits that are hard to reach, and it uproots composites of material that have been stagnant and accumulating over a long period

of time. Once it penetrates, resurrection power begins
to elevate. It lifts us up where we belong. It lifts us up
out of our dead situations. It causes us to rise above our
circumstances and to soar on the wings of an eagle.
Believers don't have to stay down long because the
power of the living God elevates. So many of us right
now are chained and bound to the deceitfulness of this
world. We're in bondage to old traditions, to old habits,
and to false beliefs. But the power of the Gospel eman-
cipates. It's able to set us free. And he whom the Son
sets free is free indeed.

The kind of power I'm talking about confronts wickedness and overcomes every kind of evil. This is the kind
of power that Paul says the Kingdom of God is all about.
It's not about church membership—it's about power. It's
not about your Sunday morning performance or your
Wednesday night attendance. It doesn't matter how
long you've been holding down a certain position in the
church, it's about God's power working through you to
bring about a change for the Kingdom's sake. No
change equals no power. Jesus said I've already given
you the power that you need over all the power of the
enemy, and nothing by any means shall harm you. (See
Luke 10:19.)

That sounds like some good news to me. Certainly that
kind of power is worth shouting about. But, there is also
a danger here. We end up doing great spiritual harm

when we take off with what we want to hear without receiving a complete revelation from the Lord. You see, we can't afford to overlook the conjunctive adverb at the beginning of verse twenty. The King James version of the Bible says "Notwithstanding"; *The Living Bible* reads "However"; *The Good News Bible* says "But"; the *New Revised Standard* version says "Nevertheless." In spite of all the power that you possess—lest you forget, lest you become lifted up in pride, lest you get your priorities all mixed up, lest you begin to think more highly of yourself than you ought to think—the Lord wants us to know that the real source of our joy and rejoicing is not in the power that we possess, but in the blessed assurance that when the roll is called up yonder and the books shall open, we can rejoice that our names have been written in the Lamb's Book of Life.

If we want to shout about something, let's shout about the Gospel, for it is the power of God unto salvation. It ought to be easy to shout when we take a little time out to really assess our own unrighteousness and unworthiness. It was God's grace, His amazing grace, that reached way down into the muck and mire and lifted us up by His unconditional love. Now that's something to shout about. He adopted us into His family and made us joint heirs with Christ Jesus. That entitles us to all spiritual blessings in heavenly places. So if you're going to shout about something, shout about that! We are children of the king; we are more than conquerors; we are the righteousness of God. Saved, sanctified, and filled with the Holy Ghost. Shout about that! For God so loved the world and Jesus paid it all. There is, therefore, now no condemnation for them that believe. His promises are worth shouting about. His Word is worth shouting about. His great love for sinners is worth shouting about because while we were yet in our sins, Christ died for us all—the just for the unjust. The holy for the unholy. The righteous for the unrighteous. And He got up with all power in His hands. That's worth shouting about. That's a good reason to rejoice.

The Wisdom Of
A Honeybee

Judges 4:1-9

There's a recurring theme running throughout the Book of Judges—that the people of God "again did evil in the sight of the Lord." It's distressing and disturbing that the faithfulness of the Children of Israel was merely a passing thing—it comes and it goes. There's a vicious cycle of sin and evil, followed by repentance and deliverance. And it's a sad commentary of us that we have to sink into a state of hopelessness and despair before we really cry out unto our God. It's sad that we have to get to the end of our ropes, and realize that we're headed for a bottomless pit, before we can remember who we are and whose we are. It's a disturbing fact that we keep repeating our past failures, our past sins, over and over in spite of God's goodness and His clear commandments and warnings of judgment. Again and again, we continue to do evil in the sight of God.

But God does not change. He is faithful to His Word. His mercy is from everlasting to everlasting. And we find throughout the Book of Judges that when His children humbled themselves, sought His face, turned from their wicked ways and cried out unto Him out of a broken and contrite spirit, God raised up a deliverer to bring His people out of bondage and to restore peace in the land. However, after the death of each of these spiritual leaders, we discover history repeating itself; for time and time again the people did evil in the sight of the Lord. So it's not surprising that verse one of Chapter Four announces the death of yet another leader, followed by the backslidden condition of Israel.

We should never underestimate the power of godly influence. I'm sure that you've heard many testimonies about how believers have started out on this Christian journey because of the godly influence of a mother or a grandmother—who saw to it that their children went to Sunday School and BTU (Baptist Training Union); who kept the family together; who kept their children out of trouble and taught them about responsibility, by giving them chores to do; and who offered up prayers on their behalf. Many of these children could write a chapter in their own life story that begins, "But after mama died, all hell broke loose in the family, and slowly but surely I found myself getting farther and farther away from God."

When Ehud died, all hell broke loose in Israel. Bondage and oppression and misery marked the life of His chosen people, who had shown no gratitude toward their God. And when they withdrew from God, God withdrew Himself from them and sold them over into the hand of Jabin, the king of Canaan, and Sisera, the commander of the king's army. Things were so bad now that people had to sneak around from village to village by way of the back roads. Men were hunted down like animals. Women were raped, and workers had to go underground or in hideaway caves, just to thrash out a living.

For twenty years these chosen people, this royal priesthood, this holy nation sank deeper and deeper into the pit of desperation and despair. Now, all they could do was to look up and cry out. And their cries reached the throne room of the God of their salvation. This time the Lord raised up a woman to lead them out of their bondage and to restore peace to the land. Who can discern the mind of God? For His ways are not our ways and His thoughts are far above our thoughts. Surely we must know that God's strength is made perfect in human weakness. Paul says that He has chosen the foolish things of the world to confound the wise, and the weak things to confound the things which are mighty so that the world would understand that "it's not by might, nor by power, but by my Spirit says the Lord." The Lord just has a way of choosing weak things to accomplish His purpose: weak things, like Gideon (one of the least of the tribe of Manasseh), to lead an army of three hundred soldiers, armed with lamps, pitchers, and trumpets. Weak things—like Samson, who was wild and impulsive. God chooses weak things—like David, who was not able to control his passions. Weak things—like Jonah, who wanted to sit out under a tree and die. Weak things—like Elijah, who called down fire from heaven. So why wouldn't He ordain strength in the hands of a woman? "Not by might, nor by power, but by my Spirit says the Lord of Hosts."

So God prepared this weaker vessel to glorify His name, to be the heroine of the hour, and her name is Deborah, which means honeybee. A honeybee is a hard worker driven by wisdom and purpose and a strong sense of community. And this industrious, productive, and highly organized community was centered around a queen bee (not a king bee), who directed the labor force, as well as the army. In His infinite wisdom, God raised up a woman who came on the scene cloaked in the mystery and dichotomy of her own name: honeybee—sweet, but dangerous; soothing, yet powerful; with the beauty of a dove, but with the venom and sting of a serpent—truly a force to be reckoned with.

It's important that we do not overlook the fact that this woman of God did not rise to a place of prominence and power on her own. She didn't usurp any of her authority from a man, nor did she obtain it by the cunning and craftiness of men. Deborah didn't get to be judge by popular election. She didn't resort to political favors or social connections. She didn't plot or scheme or manipulate things in order to move herself up. It's God who raises up, and it's God who brings us down. The Lord uses whom He chooses, no matter who it might be. If we would just humble ourselves before God, we can be assured that when God guides, He also provides. And when God calls, He also equips. He gives you what you need, every time you need it. So then we find that God has raised up a honeybee to be the fifth judge in Israel, and to deliver His people at a time, when men tried to do what was right in their own eyes.

Don't misunderstand my purpose in presenting Deborah. I'm not an advocate of women's rights. I don't hold the position that women are superior to men, and I will never attempt to use God's Word to promote an uprising or a takeover of society by women. But I just want to present Deborah as a woman who was bold enough to take a stand for the Lord, His will, and His way; and she did, in the wisdom and power of unity.

In verse four, one of the things we learn about this honeybee is that she was a wife. And if we remember the custom and culture of the Jews at this time, we might expect a wife to be at home, while the husband is out doing the ruling and the judging. But not so in the case of Deborah. This woman was born to lead, ordained by God to lead, given the opportunity to lead, respected by the people as a capable and competent leader, and one who fully understood the expectations of her God. You see, before we can qualify for leadership in His church God expects there to be unity in the home. Deborah was a strong woman, but that doesn't mean that she was the master in her own house. The strength of a woman does not automatically imply the weakness of her man. In fact, it takes an even stronger man to recognize the God-given abilities of his wife, and then be willing to allow her the opportunities to cultivate her gifts and to reach her God-given potential. I believe it takes an even stronger man to encourage rather than discourage; to support her and not tear her down; and to recognize the truth that God's calling will never contradict with His principles of spiritual authority.

Lapidoth had to have been a strong man—not intimidated by the intelligence and skill of his companion. And in order to promote unity in the home, both husband and wife must have a clear understanding of their spiritual roles, and not get them mixed up. There's a precious relationship between submission and authority. True authority comes by way of submission. In order to get over, we have to first get under God-ordained authority, in every aspect of our lives. A wise woman knows that there is power in submission. God's power works through us only to the extent that we line ourselves up to the will and command of our God. So we can't expect to move out to places of leadership in the church or authority in the community, when we have not first submitted ourselves to the leadership and authority that God has already placed in our homes. Deborah took her first stand for unity in the home, and God exalted her to be the leader of His people.

Deborah was wise enough as a leader to understand and respect the absolute necessity of unity among the leaders. Even though she was in the number one position, wisdom told her that the Lord did not intend for her to carry out this task alone. She was wise enough to recognize her own limitations. And she was secure enough to be able to share some of the responsibility. The unity of the church is destroyed by leaders who try to hoard everything to themselves. It's a sign of selfishness, and greed, and hunger for power, when a leader refuses to acknowledge and make use of the gifts that God has anointed and placed within his reach; to call out for help in getting the job done; and then to empower the right people to do it and to give them the freedom to do it well. God has given the vision to Deborah, but He has also given her the insight and the wisdom to know that this vision is not about her. It's all about God. And when we lose sight of the whole mission of Kingdom work and begin to focus upon ourselves, we become disqualified and unfit for God to use us in His Kingdom.

This woman was not concerned about who would get the credit or who was in charge. She was not concerned about protecting her turf or whether her name appeared on the program. It was not her concern to select only her friends and family members to do the job. It was not important to her whether it was a man or another woman. She was only concerned about selecting the person who was most qualified and capable for the position, so that there would be unity in carrying out the mission. And she fully understood that unity in the church must begin at the top.

And so, Deborah and Barak (whose name means lightning) were united in their efforts. They made a good spiritual team—a man and a woman, working together for the cause of Christ, with one gift complementing the other. He couldn't make it without her head, and she couldn't make it without his hands. Deborah could not lead the army and Barak could not prophesy, but this was no time to get into squabbles over spiritual gifts and no time to debate about whose gift was superior. For we are all members one of the same Body, and all the members don't have the same function. The hand can't make it without the eye, and the ears have no reason to compete against the nose. And the knees can't just boycott the body because they got their feelings hurt. When the enemy is attacking in the heat of spiritual conflict, we can't afford to squabble over trivial things, like who has the most seniority, whose turn it is, and what a woman is not supposed to do. Just put on your armor and get on out to the battlefield! The battle is not yours anyway, it's the Lord's.

Deborah and Barak didn't allow the spirit of competition to come between them. They knew the importance of unity. They carried out God's orders together. They moved out into enemy territory together. They climbed up the side of Mount Tabor together and scoped out the enemy camp at the foot of the mountain together. And God led them to victory because they were willing to put aside their differences and work to advance the Kingdom of God together, hand in hand and side by side. In spite of what James Brown sang years ago, this is not a man's world, and it never has been. This is God's world, and Galatians 3:28 says that in Christ, "there is neither Jew nor Greek, there is neither bond nor free, there is neither male nor female; for ye are all one in Christ Jesus."

In this day of confusion and declining morality, God is calling His people to take a stand for unity in the Body of Christ. But in order to do that, we have to decrease so that He might increase. For the sake of unity, we have to allow God to give us our appointed place in service. We have to learn to seek praises from God and not from men. For the sake of unity, we have to be willing to place the needs of the Kingdom above our own desires. We have to be willing to use what we have, and not worry about what we don't have. And whatever we do, we must do it to the glory and honor of our God.

Lightning and a honeybee came together one day in the spirit of unity, and the Lord was able to do some great and mighty things. "Not by might nor by power, but by my Spirit, says the Lord of Hosts."

References

Kenneth, Taylor, *The Living Bible.* (Wheaton, IL: Tyndale House Publishers, 1971).

New Revised Standard. (Division of Christian Education of the National Council of the Churches of Christ in the United States of America, 1989).

The Good News Bible. (New York: American Bible Society. 2001).